PUBLIC INQUIRIES

A Scholar's Engagements with the Policy-Making Process

 **UTP** insights

UTP Insights is an innovative collection of brief books offering accessible introductions to the ideas that shape our world.
Each volume in the series focuses on a contemporary issue,
offering a fresh perspective anchored in scholarship. Spanning a broad range of disciplines in the social sciences and
humanities, the books in the UTP Insights series contribute to
public discourse and debate and provide a valuable resource
for instructors and students.

For a list of the books published in this series, see page 125.

PUBLIC INQUIRIES

A Scholar's Engagements with the Policy-Making Process

Michael J. Trebilcock

UNIVERSITY OF TORONTO PRESS
Toronto Buffalo London

© University of Toronto Press 2022
Toronto Buffalo London
utorontopress.com
Printed in Canada

ISBN 978-1-4875-5115-5 (cloth)   ISBN 978-1-4875-5667-9 (EPUB)
ISBN 978-1-4875-5397-5 (PDF)

Library and Archives Canada Cataloguing in Publication

Title: Public inquiries : a scholar's engagements with the policy-making
  process / Michael J. Trebilcock.
Names: Trebilcock, M.J., author.
Series: UTP insights.
Description: Series statement: UTP insights | Includes bibliographical
  references and index.
Identifiers: Canadiana (print) 20220193665 | Canadiana (ebook) 2022019369X |
  ISBN 9781487551155 (cloth) | ISBN 9781487556679 (EPUB) |
  ISBN 9781487553975 (PDF)
Subjects: LCSH: Policy sciences – Canada. | LCSH: Policy sciences –
  Canada – Decision making. | LCSH: Policy sciences – Canada –
  Decision making – Case studies. | LCGFT: Case studies.
Classification: LCC JL86.P64 T74 2022 | DDC 320.60971 – dc23

We wish to acknowledge the land on which the University of Toronto Press
operates. This land is the traditional territory of the Wendat, the Anishnaabeg,
the Haudenosaunee, the Métis, and the Mississaugas of the Credit First Nation.

University of Toronto Press acknowledges the financial support of the
Government of Canada, the Canada Council for the Arts, and the Ontario Arts
Council, an agency of the Government of Ontario, for its publishing activities.

Canada Council
for the Arts
Conseil des Arts
du Canada

ONTARIO ARTS COUNCIL
CONSEIL DES ARTS DE L'ONTARIO
an Ontario government agency
un organisme du gouvernement de l'Ontario

Funded by the   Financé par le
Government   gouvernement
of Canada   du Canada

Canada

FSC
www.fsc.org

MIX
Paper from
responsible sources
FSC® C016245

Contents

PART B: PERSONAL REFLECTIONS ON ENGAGEMENTS WITH THE WORLD OF IDEAS AND INTERESTS IN PUBLIC INQUIRIES

PART C: LESSONS LEARNED (THE HARD WAY)

Acknowledgments

I am indebted to Ben Alarie, David Beatty, Daniele Bertolini, Bruce Chapman, Ron Daniels, Tony Duggan, David Dyzenhaus, Martin Friedland, Andrew Green, Rob Prichard, Kent Roach, and anonymous reviewers for comments on earlier drafts, and to Monica Layarda and Francesco Ducci for invaluable research assistance.

PUBLIC INQUIRIES

A Scholar's Engagements with the Policy-Making Process

Introduction

For much of my more than half century career as a legal scholar and academic, I have been intrigued by the role of legal and other scholars in the policy-making process and have indeed lived much of my academic life at the intersection of ideas, interests, and institutions in the formulation of public policy. These intersections have included membership of a three-person academic committee at the Adelaide Law School, commissioned by the state attorneys-general of Australia, to evaluate the current regulation of consumer credit transactions and propose reforms thereof in the late 1960s, which led over a protracted thirty-year period to the adoption of uniform state consumer credit legislation in Australia and finally in 2009 a federal uniform statute.[1] Subsequently, on moving to the McGill Law School in Canada in the late 1960s and then the University of Toronto Law School in the early 1970s I became engaged in various capacities in a nearly two-decade process of reform of Canadian competition laws.[2] In recognition of the thinness of my initial university education in New Zealand – an undergraduate degree in law, half of it part-time while articling, and taught mainly by practitioners – in the mid-1970s I decided to retool by taking an intensive summer course in law and economics at the University of Rochester followed by a half-year fellowship in law and economics at the University of Chicago, which led to the launch (with former student, colleague, later dean and university president Rob Prichard) of the Law and Economics Program at the University of Toronto Law School in 1976 (which continues to thrive to the present day). In the late 1970s I was appointed research director of a provincial committee of inquiry into the regulation of several professions (law, accountancy, architecture, and engineering), which over a thirty-year period led to major reforms in the regulation of public accountancy in Ontario and more minor reforms to the regulation of the other professions.[3] In the early 1980s, during a sabbatical leave, I was appointed by the prime minister of Papua New Guinea as a member of a small task force to make recommendations on reform of customary property rights in land[4] (leading to an enduring interest in the field of law and development). During the 1980s I played more minor roles as a background researcher to a federal reference to the Economic Council of Canada on regulatory reform,[5] to provincial commissions of inquiry into the regulation of asbestos[6] and reform of the automobile accident compensation regime,[7] a federal royal commission on Canada's future economic prospects,[8] and in the early 1990s a federal royal commission on new reproductive technologies.[9] In the mid-1990s I served as research director of a provincial committee of inquiry into the reform of the legal aid regime in Ontario,[10] which shortly led to major institutional reforms of the regime and ten years later led in turn to my appointment by the attorney general of Ontario to undertake a one-person review of the efficacy of these reforms and to evaluate the case for further reforms.[11] In the late 1990s, I served as the research director of a multi-stakeholder provincial committee on reform of the electricity sector in Ontario, which, following a change of government, unfortunately largely failed to realize its policy objectives, ushering in a period of ad hoc policy-making in this sector that persists to this day.[12] In the early 2000s I served as a research director of a government task force on the future role of government in Ontario that had little demonstrable impact on subsequent discrete areas of policy-making.[13]

Along the way, I have sometimes appeared as an expert witness in complex competition law and regulatory matters and more recently as an expert witness for the federal government in a constitutional reference on the validity of federal legislation to create a national securities regulator, which the Supreme Court of Canada largely rejected, leaving Canada as the only developed country in the world without a national securities regulator.[14]

Thus, my record of engagement in public policy-making over a long career is scarcely an unalloyed story of the triumph of ideas over vested interests and unresponsive institutions, but very much a mixed balance sheet of successes, failures, and long slogs. It is this body of personal experience in policy-making that in part animates the following reflections.

However, I should confess at the outset to at least a qualified instrumental or consequential perspective on law and law and policy reform, as opposed to a purely internal perspective on law. I illustrate the difference in perspectives with the following account of a hallway conversation many years ago with a colleague who is a distinguished proponent of a corrective justice or internal perspective on private law, especially tort law. Corrective justice requires morally culpable injurers to compensate innocent victims for the consequences of their wrongdoing, abstracting from the efficacy of tort law in deterring accidents more generally or compensating victims of accidents more generally. I asked him whether he would support a New Zealand–style no-fault accident compensation scheme for victims of accidents, to which he replied that as a citizen he might support it, but as a scholar he would continue to argue that whatever domain was left to tort law should be governed by corrective justice principles. For me, this response was deeply unsettling: after all, for most people contemplating the impact of a potential accident on their lives, two concerns are likely to be paramount: how to prevent it from happening, and if it happens how to mitigate the health and financial consequences of it. Both sets of issues implicate a wide range of policy options well beyond tort law whose efficacy requires comparative evaluation. To treat these two issues as beyond one's remit as a tort scholar – that is, the appropriate domain for tort law – is to disengage from broader policy debates surrounding both sets of issues which an instrumental perspective is well placed to engage with, taking seriously the incentive structures of the actors in the private and public sectors, which is its distinctive focus. But I leave the defence of an internal or intrinsic perspective on law to those who subscribe to it, at least in the private law context.[15]

In part A of this book, I review theories of the role of ideas and interests in policy-making and the institutional fora where ideas and interests meet in shaping public policy.

In part B, I recount my lived experiences of engagement in public policy-making, and some lessons I have learned from various engagements.

. In part C, I attempt to draw together more general lessons from lived experience about the role of ideas, interests, and institutions in Canadian public policy-making, especially public inquiries.

PART A

The Role of Ideas, Interests, and Institutions in the Canadian Policy-Making Process

Ideas and Interests in Shaping Public Policy

Adopting, for the purposes of the following discussion, the perspective of a law and economics scholar, I distinguish two very different traditions in economic scholarship more generally and in law and economics scholarship in particular. The first tradition – a welfare economics perspective – purports to demonstrate, often empirically, that in many, even most, areas of public policy-making, governments have adopted policies that do not maximize social welfare. This literature is replete with studies that purport to show that existing policies – for example, environmental and health and safety regulation, price and entry controls, trade restrictions, agricultural subsidies and supply management schemes, and tax expenditures – often reduce social welfare. The implication of these studies seems to be that these welfare-reducing policy choices reflect the stupidity or venality of policy-makers. Once the facts are revealed, it appears to be assumed that stupidity will give way to enlightenment, or that venality, i.e., capture of policy-makers by rent-seeking special interest groups, will be repulsed by an informed and aroused public. In many respects, this perspective's assumption that better policy-making needs only better information or better ideas often reflects a naive view of policy-making, given the long-standing resistance of many of these policies to change, despite recurring criticism from welfare economists.[1]

The second tradition – an austere public choice perspective that I and my co-authors adopted in our 1982 report, *The Choice of Governing Instruments* for the Economic Council of Canada's Regulation Reference, and single-mindedly applied to public inquiries; taxation, expenditures, and debt management; state-owned enterprises, and regulation in Canada[2] – views existing policy choices as reflecting a political equilibrium among affected interests, politicians, bureaucrats, and regulators and assumes that no more economically efficient policy outcome is politically achievable. To attain or retain political office, politicians will find it rational to fashion policies that exploit political asymmetries: between marginal voters, i.e., uncommitted voters in swing electorates and infra-marginal voters; between well-informed and ill-informed voters who are vulnerable to largely symbolic policies; and between concentrated and diffuse interest groups facing differential political mobilization costs (collective action problems). Moreover, working within short electoral cycles, politicians will favour policies with immediate and visible benefits that defer costs or render them less visible, e.g., by moving them off budget. Bureaucrats will be motivated to promote policies that maximize their power, pay, and prestige. Regulators will seek a quiet life by coming to accommodations with the interests they are supposed to be regulating and perhaps also by enhancing their prospects of employment in the regulated industry after their tenure as regulators, i.e., the "capture theory" of regulation. In order to maximize readership or viewing audiences, the media will trivialize complex policy issues, rely on ready-made sources of information, sensationalize mishaps that may not reflect systemic policy failures, and turn over issues at a rapid rate with minimal investigative follow-up in order to cater to readers' and viewers' limited attention spans, i.e., rational ignorance.

According to this view, welfare economists are mostly engaged in wishful thinking and utopianism – we are already doing the best we can in a world not populated by angels. In retrospect, this view seems excessively pessimistic in attributing decisive influence to special interests and "iron triangles" of politicians, bureaucrats, and special interests on the prospects for policy improvements, as evidenced by numerous instances of significant policy changes surrounding us that this perspective often has difficulty explaining.[3]

This supports a third view of the policy-making process – more optimistic than the public choice perspective and less optimistic than the welfare economics perspective – which suggests that particular constellations of ideas, interests, and institutions under certain conditions can generate significant policy changes and improvements. It is this view to which I now turn by critiquing each of the other perspectives.

From a welfare economics perspective, the social welfare function is simply an aggregation of the utility functions or preferences of the citizens comprising the society in question. This aggregation function has been critiqued from a number of perspectives. First, Arrow's impossibility theorem demonstrated that under a wide range of conditions an aggregation of individual utility functions is often unstable and reflects welfare judgments that no majority of citizens would support. Second, individual utility functions and their intensity are seldom directly observable or measurable, leading to crude proxies for welfare judgments such as the impact of a given policy on GDP per capita. However, such proxies will clearly miss or discount many sources of human utility or disutility. Third, even if these problems can be overcome or mitigated, the essentially utilitarian foundation of social welfare judgments raises serious normative issues as to the appropriate scope and salience of majority welfare versus minority welfare as affected by various policy choices. While Kaplow and Shavell[4] argue that fairness concerns can be captured in the social welfare calculus (minorities with intense preferences will be weighed appropriately in the welfare calculus), as noted above, intensity of preferences is often not directly observable and even if it were possible, majority preferences may override those of even intense minorities, raising concerns of a tyranny of the majority. This problem is rendered more acute in liberal democracies where, in principle, citizens as electors are each entitled to one vote, whatever the intensity of their preferences in policy options. Hence, we observe in many liberal democracies entrenched bills of rights protecting specified individual rights against majoritarian encroachment (and in this respect requiring recognition of a role for intrinsic normative values that are immune from a utilitarian calculus in a constitutional law context). Similarly, we observe the evolution of international human rights conventions or covenants designed to protect individual minority rights against majoritarian oppression (although entrenched protection of certain minority rights may sometimes pose opposing problems of a tyranny of the minority). None of these complexities are well captured in conventional social welfare judgments made by welfare economists in evaluating current or proposed public policies.[5]

With respect to the public choice perspective on the policy-making process, it essentially assumes an implicit market for public policies driven by the self-interest of all major actors on both the supply and demand sides of such a market, akin to explicit private markets in which the supply and demand for goods and services are resolved.[6] However, this analogy between private and political markets (at least from the benefit of hindsight) is in many respects a gross over-simplification.

First, it assumes self-interested behaviour of relevant actors, akin to profit maximization or consumer satisfaction in private markets, although it is self-evident that in many political markets, key actors, including voters at large, are motivated by a mix of inner-directed and other-directed concerns not well captured in narrow notions of rational self-interested behaviour, including notions of distributive justice, communitarianism, libertarianism, corrective justice, gender and racial equality, due process, etc. By extension, the conception of interest groups as motivated by the material self-interest of their members grossly oversimplifies the reality of interest groups or organizations in many contemporary societies. Although many interest groups are so motivated, many other interest groups are organized around non-materially self-interested values (e.g., Green Peace, Human Rights Watch, Amnesty International, the American Civil Liberties Union, Oxfam). In recent decades, in many liberal democracies, civil society groups and domestic and international NGOs, some leadership-driven, some membership-driven, have dramatically proliferated and are often important actors in the competition among interest groups and ideas that influence the public policy-making process.

Second, the rational actor model of human behaviour espoused by public choice theory and many economists often ignores the findings of recent behavioural economics scholars that many individuals in their choices often deviate from this conception of rational self-interest maximization or optimization and make choices reflecting psychological heuristics, e.g., loss aversion, the availability heuristic, anchoring, framing, confirmation bias, etc.[7]

Third, public choice theory faces difficulties in accounting for shifts in social norms. However, a complex body of scholarship, largely drawing on social psychology, demonstrates that individual and social norms are not static but evolve in response to myriad factors, sometimes leading to a new social consensus on such norms. Conversely, in other cases evolving social norms may lead to increased social and political factionalism, sometimes exacerbated by the new social media and echo chamber effects of this form of social interaction, leading in either case to demands for policy reforms that reflect these new norms (while recognizing that the law itself may sometimes serve an expressive function in shaping social norms).[8]

Fourth, while ideas and interests are clearly important determinants of public policy outcomes, they must be mediated through institutions in order to be translated into public policy. However, institutions do not suddenly appear fully formed; they have to be invented. Clearly the organization and character of institutions reflect both competing social forces that struggle to embed their interests in these institutions, and ideas about appropriate arrangements for governance. However, once institutions are adopted, they tend to exert an independent influence on what interests and ideas in particular policy domains are privileged or marginalized in subsequent public policy decisions. Moreover, once institutions have been put in place in a given society, they tend to be "sticky" and resistant to fundamental change, reflecting increasing returns, network effects, confirmation bias, and vested interests that derive perquisites from the institutional status quo, resulting in a form of path dependency.[9] Many of these institutional nuances are better captured by strands of the "new institutionalist" scholarship than public choice theory. This literature emphasizes the role of structural factors (e.g., geography, natural resources, the division of power), deeply entrenched ideational and cultural values, and cognitive heuristics and biases in constraining policy choices, or at least require framing such choices in ways that are consonant with, or at least do not contradict, these underlying constraints. "Logics of appropriateness" evolve as to what proposals may or may not credibly be advanced in particular institutional fora, and these logics condition citizens' views of feasible policy options.[10]

Austere versions of public choice theory are also largely insensitive to myriad differences in institutional arrangements for the resolution of public policy issues from one polity to another. Some political regimes are parliamentary, others presidential; some are unitary states, others federal states; some voting regimes are first past the post, some entail mandatory voting; some entail proportional representation or some combination of first past the post and proportional representation, some entail preferential, i.e., ranked voting. Some polities provide for extensive use of public referenda on contentious policy issues; others do not. Some polities have adopted bicameral legislative structures, others unicameral. Bicameral structures themselves vary widely, with membership of some upper houses determined by government appointment, in others by popular election but with the electoral franchise differing sharply from that applicable to the lower house. Some upper houses have extensive powers, others modest powers. Some polities heavily regulate expenditures on lobbying and campaign financial contributions or even publicly subsidize the latter, while other jurisdictions adopt minimal constraints on such expenditures. Some jurisdictions have extensive written constitutions, including entrenched bills of rights that assign significant oversight responsibilities to superior courts, while other jurisdictions assign a less central role to written constitutions, bills of rights, and judicial oversight thereof. In some jurisdictions written constitutions are relatively easy to amend or opt out of, others much more difficult. In some jurisdictions courts are relatively independent of the executive and legislative arms of government and judicial appointments are relatively non-politicized, while in other jurisdictions courts are less independent and more politicized. In some jurisdictions public policy development is delegated or assigned in important contexts to legislative committees, quasi-independent regulatory agencies, executive agencies of government, law reform commissions, commissions of inquiry, advisory panels, committees, or task forces appointed or constituted by the legislative or executive arms of government. In other jurisdictions this delegation function exhibits a quite different institutional matrix.

Ideas, including those of scholars, technical expertise, social norms, interests, votes, and money are likely to have very different currencies and rates of exchange in these widely different institutional fora for public policy development, including proposals to reform or shift the institutional fora where these issues are being addressed. This issue is the focus of much of the balance of this volume, partly drawing on my own career experiences noted briefly in the introduction, and partly drawing on a broader and diverse scholarly literature.

Where Ideas and Interests Intersect: Mapping the Policy-Making Terrain

An Overview

Reflecting the *sui generis* structure of institutional arrangements that shape public policy formation in different polities, in this section I briefly map these arrangements in the jurisdiction that I know best: Canada. In such a mapping exercise, it is useful to distinguish, albeit somewhat arbitrarily, inputs and outputs of the policy-making process. Outputs, on the one hand, are likely to include legislation, regulations, guidelines, or simply executive decisions that reflect shifts in policy of the government of the day. Inputs, on the other hand, are likely to encompass myriad influences on a government's policy formation processes. At a legislative level, these are likely to include the governing party's electoral platforms, key policy commitments by the prime minister and his or her political and bureaucratic policy advisors, Cabinet discussions, debates in Parliament, questions raised by opposition members in Question Period, and deliberations of standing and select parliamentary committees. This legislative activity may in turn be prompted by a wide range of sources, including public opinion polls, focus groups, investigative reporting by mainstream media of policy failures or deficiencies; intense constellations of concern that emerge in social media; studies by think tanks or academics; agitation or briefs or lobbying by private interest groups or civil society associations, or litigation in the courts raising constitutional or administrative law challenges or class actions alleging government failures of one kind or another.

Donald Savoie[11] has described an increasing tendency in recent decades in Canada (and elsewhere) to centralize key policy-making initiatives and senior civil service appointments in the office of the prime minister and his political "courtiers" (in Savoie's terms) (a trend often observable also in provincial government policy-making) and to downgrade the role of Cabinet, Parliament, and parliamentary committees in the policy-making process (at least in majority governments).

Beyond legislative activity, many outputs of contemporary public policy formation take the form of regulations or guidelines promulgated by executive branches of government or regulatory agencies constituted by government to regulate particular spheres of activity. Much contemporary legislation contemplates extensive delegation to executive or regulatory arms of government in elaborating the details of legislative mandates. The exercise of this delegated function may be dispositive, may take the form of recommendations to ministers or Cabinet, may be subject to Cabinet appeal, or may be subject to ministerial directives.

Beyond agencies of government charged with elaborating the details of delegated legislation, governments sometimes set up permanent or semi-permanent public policy–oriented research institutions, such as standing law reform commissions or scientific or economic advisory agencies. Other standing institutions of government may also exert significant influence on policy formation, including auditors general, ombudspersons, human rights commissioners, freedom of information commissioners, and parliamentary budget officers, among others.

I comment briefly on standing policy advisory bodies and parliamentary committees before turning to more extended comments on ad hoc public inquiries (commissions of inquiries and ad hoc government task forces).[12] I focus on these policy-making fora because these are where academics are likely to be most actively engaged.

Standing and Semi-permanent Policy Advisory Bodies

Here I have in mind bodies such as the Economic Council of Canada and the Law Commission of Canada, both charged with providing policy advice to the federal government within their expansive mandates. Both have had a chequered history.

The Economic Council of Canada was established in 1963 and operated under various distinguished chairs, making policy recommendations by internal consensus of its members. It was disbanded by the Mulroney government in 1992 after it published a report that suggested that the separation of Quebec from Canada would be unlikely to have the dire economic consequences that many predicted.

The Law Reform Commission of Canada was established in 1971. No legislation based on its recommendations was enacted during its first ten years of existence. It was disbanded in 1992. It was re-established as the Law Commission of Canada in 1996, but the Harper government terminated its funding in 2006. It released two controversial reports in its brief existence – one proposing abolition of restrictions on same-sex marriage, and another proposing a mixed-member proportional representation regime for parliamentary elections (both arguably beyond the competence and credibility of a lawyer-dominated body).

It is not difficult to discern the challenges facing such bodies. If, on the one hand, within their typically expansive mandates they choose of their own motion to explore contentious policy issues, they risk antagonizing governments apprehensive about losing control of their policy agenda. If, on the other hand, they only pursue policy issues on referral by governments, governments face the risk of remitting issues to bodies whose composition has been established prior to such referrals and may not reflect the expertise or legitimacy that the policy issue in question demands, while their established internal decision-making and public consultation processes may not be well adapted to the issues in question. Ad hoc public inquiries permit the government greater control over agendas, key personnel, and decision-making and public participation processes.

Parliamentary Committees

Parliamentary committees have been a long-standing feature of policy-making in Canada at both the federal and provincial levels. Federally, there are twenty-four standing committees, one special committee, and one liaison committee of the House of Commons, eighteen standing committees of the Senate, and two joint standing committees.[13]

Typically, legislation proposed by the government of the day will be referred to the relevant standing committee after second reading. Occasionally, bills will be referred to standing committees after first reading, and sometimes Green or White Papers will be referred to parliamentary committees, indicating a range of policy options on particular issues or government policy preferences on these issues, but leaving committees greater scope for policy inputs than in bills referred to committees after second reading. In some cases, select committees will be constituted to study particular issues of contemporary policy salience. In all cases, committees report to the House of Commons, including any proposed amendments to pending legislation.

Parliamentary committees have a very mixed record of policy impact.[14] Chairs of these committees are appointed by the government of the day and often serve very short tenures. The composition of the committees typically reflects the proportion of seats held in the House of Commons by various political parties (and subject commonly to tight party discipline), and in the case of majority governments, is dominated by backbenchers from the party constituting the government. Historically, committees have received thin staff support – usually a non-partisan clerk – and have access to the research resources of the Library of Parliament but have limited capacity to commission research of their own, which must be financed out of each committee's regular budget. Committee studies often lack a clearly defined focus and adequate follow-up mechanisms.[15] While committees can order the appearance of witnesses and the production of documents, the enforcement of these orders must be referred to the House as a whole.[16] Typically, witnesses before parliamentary committees are either invited to appear by the committee or request the opportunity to make representations. In both cases, witnesses may include academics.

At the provincial level, practice with legislative committees varies substantially from one province to another, but a general concern is that such committees are often very ad hoc in nature, with large and floating membership, significant absenteeism, late substitution of members before meetings, and weak staff and research support.[17]

Ad Hoc Commissions of Inquiry

Historical Origins
A commission of inquiry is a body created by a government under the federal *Inquiries Act* or the corresponding provincial or territorial statute.[18] Commissions of inquiry have long been a central feature of the Canadian public policy-making

process. Their history can be traced back to their frequent use in the colony by the British government long before Confederation. Indeed, the impetus for the union of Upper and Lower Canada into a single colony with a British-style parliamentary system originated from the report authored by governor-general and royal commissioner, Lord Durham, in 1838.[19]

Between 1876 and 1900 alone, the Canadian government established on average two public inquiries every year.[20] A total of 450 federal inquiries have been commissioned under the *Inquiries Act* between Confederation and 2014 – averaging three commissions per year,[21] and many more at the provincial level, probably in aggregate numbering around 2000 (although there is no official count of provincial commissions).

Legal Basis of Commissions of Inquiry

Commissions of inquiry may be established by the executive arm of the federal, provincial, or territorial government. Each level of government has constitutional authority to establish a public inquiry relating to a subject matter that falls under its competent area of jurisdiction.

The federal *Inquiries Act*[22] is strikingly concise. It empowers and confers broad discretion to the Governor in Council (Cabinet) to initiate any investigations "concerning any matter connected with the good government" or the conduct of "public business" in Canada.[23] In essence, Cabinet can form a commission of inquiry into virtually anything it deems expedient. All provincial and territorial governments have their own versions of public inquiry statutes, which bear a structural and substantive resemblance to the federal statute. However, some provincial and territorial statutes, such as the Ontario *Public Inquiries Act*, set out more detailed rules governing commissions of inquiry than their federal counterpart. Section 5 of the Ontario statute, for instance, expressly outlines the commission's duty of honesty, impartiality, proportionality, and fiscal responsibility.[24] The relatively more modern Ontario statute also sets out in more detail the rules of evidence applicable to proceedings held by the commission, including rules governing admissibility, privilege, and confidentiality, which are absent from the federal statute.[25]

In all cases, the public inquiries statutes give commissioners wide-ranging powers, including the power to summons documents and compel testimony under oath[26] and to engage the assistance of counsel, experts, and assistants in conducting an inquiry.[27] The statutes also provide basic procedural requirements to protect individual rights and procedural fairness: any individuals who may be subject to certain charges or allegations have a right to reasonable notice[28] and a right to be represented by counsel to allow the person to make representations or rebuttals before the commission.[29]

Once the government decides to appoint a commission of inquiry, the government specifies the mandate, or formally known as the terms of reference, of a commission of inquiry in the Order in Council. The terms of the reference are legally binding. The government may also determine the date on which a report is to be submitted to the government. Acting outside the terms of reference leads to the commission acting without jurisdiction and, therefore, illegally.[30] Terms of reference will usually specify whether the commission is mandated to conduct fact-finding or to review and recommend policies or both.[31]

Canadian courts have generally afforded significant deference to commissioners in determining the appropriate procedures to conduct public inquiries.[32] However, on occasions, courts have played a role in ensuring the independence and impartiality of commissions of inquiry and the legality of their conduct in reference to the governing statute and their terms of reference. In the past, courts have declared void parts of a commission's findings on the ground that the commissioner behaved in a biased manner[33] or violated fundamental principles of fairness, such as by failing to give an affected party adequate notice.[34]

Forms of Inquiries

The *Inquiries Act* traditionally contemplates two primary functions of inquiry: policy advisory and investigatory. Advisory commissions of inquiry typically have broad mandates to address specified issues of public policy and provide recommended policy prescriptions. The second form of inquiry has a more retrospective investigatory and fact-finding outlook. Investigatory commissions tend to have a narrower mandate to study matters of controversy that are precipitated by a public tragedy or wrongdoing, including past actions by the government and its representatives. Most commissions, however, defy easy categorization, and the line between advisory and investigatory inquiries is frequently blurred as commissions take on a hybrid role. One legal scholar has aptly remarked that virtually every commission turns into a policy commission because investigative commissions contextualize their mandate in a broader policy environment and frequently make wide-ranging policy recommendations.[35]

Frequency and Sectoral Scope of Commissions of Inquiry

The circumstances leading to the appointment of a commissioner are "as varied as the exigencies of political life."[36] In terms of their sectoral breadth, commissions of inquiry have touched on virtually every major policy sector in Canada. The following list provides examples of prominent advisory federal inquiries based on their relevant policy areas:

(i)   Security and defence: Royal Commission on the Defence of Canada (1861); the Royal Commission on Security (1966)

(ii)   Federalism: Royal Commission on Dominion-Provincial Relations (1937–40)

(iii)   Public administration: Royal Commission on Government Organization (1960); Royal Commission on Electoral Reform and Party Financing (1989)

(iv)   Fiscal, economic, and trade policy: Royal Commission on Taxation (1962); Royal Commission on Canada's Economic Prospects (1955); Royal Commission on Banking and Finance (1961)

(v)   Infrastructure: Royal Commission on Railways (1887); Royal Commission on Transportation (1959)

(vi)   Law: Royal Commission to Investigate the Penal System of Canada (1938); Royal Commission on the Revision of the Criminal Code (1949)

(vii)   Environment and natural resources: Royal
        Commission on Energy (1957); Royal Commission
        on Seals and the Sealing Industry in Canada (1984)
(viii) Public health: Royal Commission on Health Services
        (1961); Royal Commission on the Future of Health
        Care in Canada (2001)
  (ix) Crown-Indigenous relations: Royal Commission on
        Aboriginal Peoples (1991); National Inquiry into Missing
        and Murdered Indigenous Women and Girls (2016)
  (x)   Other socio-cultural issues: Royal Commission on
        Bilingualism and Biculturalism (1963); Royal
        Commission on the Status of Women (1967)

Investigatory commissions of inquiry have also been
employed in varied circumstances and often politically vol-
atile areas ranging from investigation into an airplane crash
and airplane bombing[37] to investigation into allegations of
misconduct by the armed forces and allegations of bribery
of public officials.[38]

The provinces have launched similarly high-profile public inquiries. The recommendations of Ontario's Inquiry
into Pediatric Forensic Pathology in Ontario led to an institutional rearrangement of forensic pathology service in the
province and has had a major impact on the development
of the Canadian law of evidence, especially in respect to
expert evidence.[39] The Nova Scotia government formed
the Westray Mine Public Inquiry to investigate the mining
explosion that killed twenty-six miners in the Westray Mine
and to make recommendations to avert future mining disas-
ters. The report prompted amendments of the *Criminal Code*

for the purpose of establishing corporate liability for workplace deaths and injuries.[40]

Strengths of Commissions of Inquiry

Scholars have identified important roles that commissions of inquiry have played in the public policy process in catalysing policy change; generating new policy ideas; and educating the public and restoring public confidence.

Catalysts for Policy Change. A number of transformative policy changes in Canada can be attributed to the work of commissions of inquiry: the Royal Commission on Dominion-Provincial Relations (the "Rowell-Sirois Commission") in the 1930s led the rearrangement of taxing powers between the federal government and the provinces; the Royal Commission on Health Services (the "Hall Commission") in the 1960s led to a national medicare plan; the Royal Commission on the Economic Union and Development Prospects for Canada (the "Macdonald Commission") in the 1980s led to a continental free trade agreement with the United States; and the Commission of Inquiry on the Blood System (the "Krever Commission") in the 1990s led to the establishment of the current publicly administered national blood system.

The successes of these commissions in ushering policy changes can often be attributed in part to institutional attributes that are conducive to policy innovations. Compared to the regular policy machineries of the government, which are often siloed and face constant pressures to deal simultaneously with a plethora of current issues, commission of inquiries are mandated to focus on a particular issue and can devote time and resources to undertake a comprehensive evaluation of evidence and policy alternatives before making their final recommendations.[41] The combination of fact-finding powers and advisory function in a single commission also presents the obvious advantage of being able to form optimal recommendations with a thorough understanding of the factual matrix that gave rise to the issues of concern.[42]

Idea Generation. Commissions of inquiry present a unique environment for actors in the policy-making landscape to propose and debate ideas. Because commissions of inquiry are not bound to follow strict procedural formalities, they enjoy flexibility to structure their procedures and to conduct hearings in a manner the commissioners deem most suitable to carrying out their mandates. Policy commissions have regularly utilized non-conventional hearings in the form of "seminars," "round tables," and even "town hall meetings."[43]

Commissions of inquiry also have the institutional potential to break out of existing policy silos, enabling them to form a more holistic understanding of policy problems that defy easy categorization. Indeed, they have often been employed to address issues that cannot be singularly captured by existing departments or branches of government. For instance, women's issues, which were the focus of the Royal Commission on the Status of Women (the "Bird Commission"), were an emerging area that cut horizontally across numerous policy areas, including gender, health, education, labour, and family law, as well as social services. The work of the commission has been credited for advancing women's issues as an independent policy area and for pushing the federal and provincial governments to construct policy machinery at the departmental level dedicated to advancing women's equality.[44] Even where commissions of inquiry have not seen a direct implementation of their policy recommendations, as in the case of the Royal Commission of Aboriginal Peoples, they may still affect long-term policy processes through idea generation and issue reframing.[45]

Promoting Public Education and Restoring Public Confidence. Finally, commissions of inquiry also play an important role in informing the public on important issues, building popular momentum for change and restoring public confidence in government processes. As the Supreme Court of Canada has noted, the "social function" that the commissions play "is probably [even] more important in the long run" than their specific policy recommendations.[46] The publicity and transparency of the inquiry process put commissions of inquiry at a structural advantage to fulfil this role. While many policy processes or investigations are conducted in private, public inquiries ordinarily attract significant media coverage which alerts the public to their operation. Public hearings may also provide concerned citizens with the opportunity to participate in the hearings or make submissions to the commission. The decision to hold the Walkerton Inquiry hearings into contaminated municipal water supply in Walkerton, Ontario, for instance, was made in part to allow members of the public who had personally been most affected by the contamination of municipal drinking water to attend the public hearings and hear the evidence directly from the relevant actors, including the chief coroner of Ontario and the manager of the Walkerton water system.[47] In the course of the Walkerton Inquiry, commission staff met with representatives of local groups, held town hall meetings to hear directly from affected local residents, and received and considered formal submissions from local groups.[48]

Critiques of Commissions of Inquiry

Commissions of inquiry, however, have not been immune from criticism. The policy-making track record of commissions of inquiry is rather mixed overall. Commissions have been criticized for exceeding the initial time and budget estimates, interpreting their mandate too broadly, and generating sweeping policy recommendations that are unrealistic and fail to account for political and fiscal feasibility.

This mirrors a similar tension for academic researchers for such commissions, and indeed academics more generally for whom there is a large academic premium in generating bold new ideas that may have major long-term implications in particular policy domains but do not attempt to resolve much more complex sets of policy trade-offs faced by the ultimate political decision-makers operating across multiple policy domains and within much shorter time frames. Whether embedding academics in the executive arm of government for extended terms, as is common in the United States on a change in administration, but uncommon in parliamentary systems (like Canada's) with a permanent civil service, is likely to produce a better integration of perspectives is an open question.[49] In turn, in the US system of divided government, ad hoc government commissions of inquiry or policy task forces are much less common than in parliamentary systems such as Canada's. Commissions of inquiry, at least in theory, offer the potential advantage of facilitating the deployment of a much richer array of academic perspectives than secondment of individual academics to government on a full-time limited-term basis.

Efficiency and Cost Effectiveness. A frequent criticism is that commissions of inquiry take too long and cost too much. While its impact on shaping Canada's future economic policy trajectory has rarely been questioned, the Macdonald Royal Commission took thirty-four months to produce its three-volume, 2000-page report at a cost of $20.6 million.[50] There have also been many instances where the commissions substantially exceeded their initial time and budget estimates. The Commission of Inquiry into the Deployment of Canadian Forces in Somalia (also known as the "Somalia Inquiry") was initially given nine months to investigate certain aspects of the deployment of Canadian peacekeeping forces to Somalia. After three extension requests and one and a half years past the original deadline, the federal government required it to wrap up its operations.[51]

Some commissions, especially those with an investigatory mandate, have been prone to become excessively bogged down in adversarial processes, which have inevitably prolonged the process and increased its cost. Delays and interruptions caused by intervening litigation are unfortunately frequent. The Somalia Inquiry became embroiled in five lengthy applications for judicial review.[52] The Cabinet's decision to wrap up the inquiry before its completion descended into a legal dispute, which was ultimately resolved by

Federal Court of Appeal that upheld the government's decision to terminate the commission's work.[53] Similar judicial review challenges, and thus additional delays and expense, also plagued the work of the Krever Commission of Inquiry,[54] Nova Scotia's Royal Commission on the Donald Marshall, Jr., Prosecution,[55] and the Royal Commission of Inquiry into the Confidentiality of Health Records,[56] among others.

Lack of Policy Implementation. While some commissions of inquiry have seen their key recommendations swiftly adopted by governments, some have not engendered such responses. There are a number of reasons that contribute to the lack of implementation. Obviously, implementation is, by design, the prerogative of the government, not the commission. The frequent time lag between the establishment and the conclusion of an inquiry often means a new government must respond to and implement the recommendations from an inquiry initiated by its predecessor. The new government may have different policy priorities and thus lack the political will and/or resources to implement the commission's recommendations or give credit to a previous government for its policy initiatives.[57]

Similarly, some commissions have recommended sweeping and costly reforms that may take years or decades for the recommendations to be implemented. Such was the case of many of the recommendations of the Royal Commission on Aboriginal Peoples. The final five-volume, 4000-page report released by the commission called for sweeping changes to the relationship between Aboriginal people, non-Aboriginal people, and governments in Canada spanning a vast range of issues including self-governance, treaties, health, housing, the north, economic development, and education. While laudable in many respects, many of these recommendations are yet to see implementation.[58] A signature recommendation for dividing the work of the Department of Indian Affairs was ultimately implemented but only after a two-decade delay.[59]

Threats to Civil Liberties. Civil libertarian objections to commissions of inquiry mostly target investigative inquiries. By design, there are fewer procedural safeguards in an inquiry than are available in a regular trial. While there are basic legal protections for civil liberties built into public inquiries statutes,[60] some critics contend that they are insufficient to allay their concerns.[61] First, the usual rules of evidence and burden of proof do not apply to inquiries and hearings conducted by the commissions.[62] Although inquiries do not carry any legal consequences, they may nevertheless have incidental legal effects. Problems such as self-incrimination may arise, given the commission's power to compel witnesses. Although evidence from public inquiries is technically inadmissible in subsequent criminal or civil proceedings, they may give the prosecution or opposing parties a tactical advantage over the affected individuals. Furthermore, regardless of the ultimate findings, individuals subjected to inquiries may incur substantial reputational damage for which they have little recourse.[63]

Vulnerability to Government Manipulation and Procrastination. Commissions of inquiry have also been criticized for their vulnerability to government manipulation and procrastination. They may, for instance, be used as a vehicle to deflect political accountability. As one commentator has observed, "Once an inquiry is set up, a government can answer embarrassing questions by saying that the matter is before an inquiry."[64] Perhaps such risk is inherent in the political nature of public inquiries. Their governing statutes empower the executive branch to set up an inquiry whenever it deems expedient, and thus the decision to create a public inquiry is inherently political.[65] Nevertheless, a consensus has largely settled on the view that commissions of inquiry are independent bodies, not merely an extension of the executive. Reports produced by commissions of inquiry have often reflected views highly critical of the government.[66] Furthermore, commissions of inquiry have ordinarily been allowed to run their course. The decision of the federal government to wind up the work of the Somalia Inquiry may be interpreted as signalling executive willingness to interfere in the work of commissions of inquiry in the future, but thus far such extreme interference in the work of a commission has remained exceptional.[67]

Ad Hoc Government Task Forces

Government task forces are a generic form of inquiry and more difficult to describe in general terms than commissions of inquiry, in that there is an even greater possible variation of form within the general mode, reflecting the dominant characteristics of task forces, which are their informality and flexibility. While there is no official count of such task forces in Canada at both the federal and provincial levels, they almost certainly exceed, by orders of magnitude, the number of formal commissions of inquiry over the country's history.

Task forces depend for their existence on informal executive appointment. They lack the legal status, powers, and constraints imposed by the *Inquiries Act*. As a result, they are generally cheaper, faster, and less formal than royal commissions, and less likely to adopt an investigative or adjudicative mode. They are generally perceived as less independent of the executive arm of government than commissions of inquiry. The membership of task forces may be drawn exclusively from a department of government, may be interdepartmental, or may combine personnel drawn from both the public and private sectors. Task forces governed by terms of reference issued either formally or informally by the responsible minister are not required by statute or convention to publish their reports or to make accessible the research on which their recommendations are based.

Obviously, the different modes of public inquiries vary along different dimensions including: how and against what criteria appointments are made to the inquiry body; the openness and transparency of a body's deliberations; the scope and nature of its consultations with or participation of affected or interested constituencies; how it goes about identifying a research agenda, including relevant normative perspectives, technical expertise and empirical evidence, and commissioning and overseeing such research and its public accessibility and dissemination; what rules govern its internal decision-making processes; and what factors influenced the outcome and impact of the inquiry.

Against this simplified mapping of the policy formation process in Canada, in the next section I review my own experiences in engaging with these institutional fora that shape the policy-making process in Canada (and briefly Australia and Papua New Guinea) and offer some necessarily tentative lessons that I have drawn from these experiences, in particular the efficacy of ad hoc public inquiries and prospects of enhancing their efficacy with particular attention directed to terms of reference; leadership; composition; and process.

Personal Reflections on Engagements with the World of Ideas and Interests in Public Inquiries

Consumer Protection Policy

In the course of my first academic appointment at the University of Adelaide Law School in the 1960s I was one of three faculty members appointed by the Standing Committee of Attorneys-General of the Commonwealth and states of Australia to undertake a critical evaluation of the current law relating to consumer credit and moneylending in the states and propose appropriate legal reforms. The chair of the committee was the dean of the law school, joined by me and another young colleague. The dean's specialization was public international law, and my colleague specialized in constitutional law and jurisprudence. I taught commercial law and corporate law. Thus, our credentials for undertaking such an evaluation were modest. However, our home state had recently elected a Labour government after decades of status quo conservative governments, led by a young, energetic, and articulate premier on a strong social reform platform and supported by several strong ministers (several of whom, including the premier, being lawyers). We began work in May 1966 and completed our report in February 1969. We undertook our assignment on a pro bono basis. While the Standing Committee of Attorneys-General was initially reluctant to release the report, the South Australian government decided to publish it of its own initiative and enacted comprehensive legislation closely based on it two years later. This precipitated similar inquiries and initiatives in other states, and over the ensuing years these initiatives led to the enactment of uniform consumer credit statutes in all the states by the mid-1980s and the enactment

of the national consumer *Credit Protection Act 2009* by trans-
fer of jurisdiction to the federal government by the states.

Professor Anthony Duggan, in a later review essay of the
evolution of consumer credit laws in Australia and elsewhere over the intervening years, has described our report
as "remarkably influential,"[1] while noting emerging phe-
nomena in consumer credit markets that present new challenges, including the dramatic proliferation of consumer
credit cards and the complexities they pose for consumers
in figuring out charges and interest rates on debits and pay-
ments, increased tendencies to overcommitment reflected in
rising personal bankruptcy rates; subprime mortgage lend-
ing; and payday loans. In an earlier retrospective twenty-
one years after our report was published, I attempted to
provide a more detailed assessment of the strengths and
weaknesses of our report, with the benefit of fifteen years
of immersion in law and economics scholarship over the
intervening years.[2] I noted that the late 1960s, in the United
States in particular, but elsewhere around the developed
world, including Australia, was a period of intense political and policy activism reflected in consumer crusades; the
emergence of a strong environmental movement; the rise
of feminism; protest movements against poverty and rac-
ism; and the beginnings of an anti-war movement. In this
political and policy environment, it was a challenge to
maintain a sense of balance and realism. For the most part, I
believe that our committee struck a reasonable balance and
resisted more extreme reform proposals, such as tight statutory interest rate ceilings on most consumer credit transactions and drastic curtailment of creditors remedies, on the

grounds that such measures were likely to exclude many consumers from consumer credit markets or force them into black markets. Much influenced by contemporary debates in the United States over truth-in-lending laws, in an environment of dramatically expanding consumer credit, we focused for the most part on addressing informational asymmetries facing consumers in consumer credit transactions and consumer markets more generally: imperfect information about the quality and characteristics of goods being provided; imperfect or deceptive information about the cost of credit; imperfect information about the terms of consumer credit agreements; and imperfect information about remedies available to consumers in the event of seller or financier delinquencies.

However, as I also noted in my retrospective evaluation of our report, we explicitly recognized that a number of our information-enhancing reform proposals were predicated on the availability of a competitive range of choices of suppliers and financiers in consumer credit markets and consumer markets more generally, and that we had neither the time nor the resources to investigate the competitive structure of most of these markets. In retrospect, I believe that this was a serious shortcoming of our report. For example, at the time of our work, banks were marginal players in consumer credit markets (before the advent of credit cards), and we should have investigated whether there were regulatory or other impediments to their entry into these markets. Indeed, subsequent research has shown that truth-in-lending laws have had a limited impact on the dispersion in consumer credit rates, either because disclosure came too late to influence consumers' decisions or because some segments of the consumer credit market are not effectively competitive.[3] Thus, one important lesson I learned from this initial foray into ad hoc policy-making processes is that facts matter, but which facts and whose facts and how should new facts be gathered? This is a theme to which I return in many of my subsequent observations in this book.

However, to put a point on this concern in the consumer protection policy context, clearly the consumer-protection policy-reform agenda has evolved significantly – in some respects dramatically – since the late 1960s. Even by the early to mid-1970s, in the United States and elsewhere, much of the reform focus had shifted from debates over truth-in-lending laws to forms of risk regulation, as exemplified by the creation of new regulatory agencies in the United States (and elsewhere) – in the United States under a Republican administration led by President Nixon, such as the Occupational Safety and Health Administration; the National Highway Traffic Safety Agency; the Consumer Product Safety Commission; and the Environmental Protection Agency – all created within a few years of each other. The appropriate role of the state and its agencies in regulating risks of one kind or another, and the relative roles of science and popular perceptions and opinions remain a matter of controversy and are reflected in the crazy quilt of regulations in most jurisdictions that reflect no consistent relationship, such as between the public and private costs of regulatory measures and the number of lives saved by these measures. While our research is now seriously outdated, I and two colleagues in the mid-1990s reviewed the extensive empirical evidence on risk regulation in various contexts, in an attempt to take the facts seriously.[4] This is a lesson that I have attempted to take seriously in all or most of my subsequent ad hoc policy reform engagements.

I note here a further afterthought from the Adelaide Law School committee experience: a central premise of the report was that consumer credit regulation hitherto had been driven by form, not function, so that different laws and regulations applied to different kinds of secured consumer credit transactions, and that any serious reform agenda should seek to apply the same legal framework to all consumer credit transactions serving the same function, irrespective of their form. For registration of security interests arising under consumer credit transactions, we suggested that they be registered, in the case of motor vehicles, with the registrar of motor vehicles in each state, but we declined to propose more sweeping reforms of personal property security laws on the grounds that many security interests in personal property were business and not consumer-related and were hence beyond our remit. However, following the lead of the United States and the adoption in most states of the Uniform Commercial Code Article 9, Australia, New Zealand, and Canada have all, over the intervening years, enacted integrated personal property security regimes, now typically in electronic form. The most dramatic exception to this trend is the United Kingdom where, despite recommendations by the Crowther Committee fifty years ago and many similar recommendations in later studies, it still does not have an integrated personal property security regime, one of the principal opponents of which has apparently been the

City of London Solicitors Association. This example raises a disquieting thought: one should not assume that lawyers either individually or collectively through their professional associations will necessarily be at the forefront of attempts to reform dysfunctional areas of law. Put at its most cynical, lawyers thrive on complexity. Complexity requires that clients consult them, and complexity drives up billable hours. In a contemporary context, with the increasing potential for ICT and AI technology to simplify many legal processes, lawyers and their professional associations have seldom been conspicuous proponents of professional regulatory reforms that would facilitate fuller utilization of these technologies by consumers or alternative service providers.[5]

Several other afterthoughts are worth brief mention because they have formed a significant focus of some of my subsequent policy reform endeavours. First, the Adelaide Law School report largely dismissed the possibility of effective private enforcement by consumers of their contractual or statutory rights and instead opted largely for a regime of public enforcement by a specialized registrar or commissioner of consumer protection. As subsequent experience has highlighted, we insufficiently explored the potential for reform of small claims courts, contingency fees, and class actions as mechanisms for facilitating private enforcement of consumer protection laws. Second, as I noted in my twenty-one-year retrospective on the Adelaide Law School report, many categories of financial instruments and services, including mortgages, insurance, pensions, annuities, disability plans, investment. and savings instruments present consumers with information problems similar to those they face in consumer credit transactions, but we regarded these classes of instruments and services as beyond our remit.[6] More generally, the increasing significance of all kinds of services in the modern economy, including professional services and ICT services, present consumers with information problems at least as challenging as those that arise in consumer credit markets.[7]

While I have emphasized the role of serendipity in the appointment of the Adelaide Law School committee, despite our modest credentials, and its relatively influential impact in the general environment of policy activism in the late 1960s and 1970s, it is salutary to reflect on the protracted nature of reform in Australia in the consumer credit domain, extending over at least a decade and a half before uniform state-level consumer credit legislation was adopted, and longer if one dates the reform to include the enactment of a national consumer credit statute. As Duggan has pointed out, at the end of this process, transformations of consumer credit markets and financial transactions more generally presented an entirely new set of policy challenges, requiring the reform process to be engaged anew.[8]

Competition Policy Reform

Upon relocating to Canada in 1969, initially to an academic appointment at McGill Law School and then in 1972 to an appointment at the University of Toronto Law School, I continued my active engagement in consumer protection policy, being elected a national vice president of the Consumers

Association of Canada in 1974 and 1975, and in that position assuming primary responsibility for a pilot program (the Regulated Industries Program), financially supported by the federal Department of Consumer and Corporate Affairs, to intervene on behalf of consumers in regulatory proceedings involving concentrated industries, including telecommunications, broadcasting, airlines, and energy, where the consumer voice had been largely absent, raising concerns about regulatory capture or at least undue influence by the industries being regulated.[9]

However, early in this period the principal policy reform focus squarely implicating the consumer interest was competition policy reform. While Canada was arguably the first country in the developed world to enact a competition law in 1889 (prior to the enactment of the US *Sherman Act* in 1890), over the ensuing decades its efficacy was largely confined to criminal sanctions for price-fixing conspiracies, but it had proven largely ineffective in addressing potentially anti-competitive mergers and abuses of dominance (monopolization), partly as a result of the criminal burden of proof and vaguely defined public interest standards applicable to mergers and abuses of dominance, and partly as a result of restrictive judicial interpretations of the prevailing provisions. In 1966, the federal government directed the newly constituted Economic Council of Canada to review Canada's competition laws and to recommend reforms. In a report released in 1969,[10] the council recommended sweeping reforms to these laws, precipitating an almost two-decade reform process, culminating in the enactment of the federal *Competition Act* in 1986. This process was characterized by abortive legislative initiatives, parliamentary committee hearings, vigorous and often acrimonious political and policy debates, and strenuous opposition to or at least serious reservations about the reform process by organized large business interests and their legal representatives. In order to placate some of this opposition, the government agreed to split the reform process into two stages, with the first stage extending the laws from goods to services, and rendering vertical practices such as tying, exclusive dealing, and refusals to deal subject to review by the Restrictive Trade Practices Commission, while postponing reform of the rules governing mergers and abuse of dominance to stage two. In order to advance the stage two amendments, the government commissioned a report by an eminent academic economist and prominent competition lawyer (the Skeoch-McDonald Report),[11] which recommended decriminalization of competition laws relating to mergers and abuses of dominance and subjecting them instead to rule of reason review by a specialized adjudicative tribunal. These recommendations were largely adopted in the stage two amendments reflected in the *Competition Act* of 1986.

I was active in the reform process over most of this period in a variety of capacities: first as a senior officer with the Consumer's Association of Canada in 1974 and 1975; as a member of an academic advisory panel to the Department of Consumer and Corporate Affairs (responsible for the administration of competition laws at the time); as director of the Law and Economics Program at the University of Toronto Law School that was launched in 1976, and as one of its major early initiatives hosted almost-yearly round tables for the ensuing decade and beyond on competition policy reform. Here members of the competition bar, senior officials from the Competition Bureau, academic lawyers, and economists could meet on neutral terrain to debate various reform proposals. Early in this period I also began co-teaching an upper-year seminar in competition law and policy with a legal colleague and an academic economist, resulting in an early book on the new legislation.[12] I continued this form of interdisciplinary academic engagement for several decades with different legal and economic co-teachers and co-authors, resulting in a much more ambitious and contemporary treatment of the subject in another book.[13] In 1987, I was appointed one of the first lay members of the newly constituted Competition Tribunal, a position from which I resigned in 1989 without a single case being referred to the tribunal, thereafter launching a significant part-time consulting practice in the competition policy field.

Looking back at this multifaceted engagement with the field, what lessons do I draw from the policy reform process? First, as with the Adelaide Law School experience and the experiences of later policy reform engagements (reviewed below), policy reform in many contexts is not for the fainthearted, the short of wind, or the impatient. Perhaps when policy reform is triggered by a major national political scandal or human disaster, public and media attention will often be sharply focused on a specific policy response to the scandal or disaster in question. But many policy reform enterprises relating to basic framework laws lack this kind of immediate political, media, and public salience and are much more likely to resemble the consumer credit and competition policy reform enterprises that I have described above. I continue to be concerned that in this kind of attritional policy reform process the voices, views, and interests of average household consumers, faced with major informational and collective actions problems, are likely to be heavily discounted – a concern that motivated the Regulated Industries Program initiative with the Consumers Association of Canada and that remains pertinent today in many policy contexts.

As to the substance of the reforms enacted, a recent retrospective review by myself and a former doctoral student Francesco Ducci[14] (with a European competition law and comparative perspective) reaches generally positive assessments of the outcome of the reform process, but notes several unresolved issues in the current legislation. First, reflecting a deficiency similar to the one I noted in the Adelaide Law School report on consumer credit, the current *Competition Act* reflects an incoherent pattern of rules on private enforcement of competition laws.[15] While the *Act* provides for private remedies for compensation in criminal offences under the *Act* (primarily cartels and misleading advertising), the decriminalization of anti-competitive mergers and abuses of dominance has deprived aggrieved parties of any remedy for compensation. As for the ability of private parties to initiate reviews of vertical practices, mergers, or abuses of dominance before the Competition Tribunal, they are permitted in vertical practices (with leave of the tribunal) but not in mergers or abuses of dominance. And in any event, any remedy is prospective only and does not entail compensation for past losses – such as in abuses of dominance. Moreover, recent amendments to the *Act* have authorized the tribunal to impose substantial administrative monetary penalties on parties found to be in violation of many of the provisions of the *Act*, which implies a form of de facto re-criminalization of practices that were intended to be merely civilly reviewable.

Second, there remains substantial unresolved jurisdictional ambiguity on the role of the Competition Bureau and industry-specific regulators in industries such as telecommunications, airlines, broadcasting, banking, and energy, particularly where the latter have engaged in partial but reversible deregulation, or where the latter are vested with jurisdiction over proposed mergers in their sectors, perhaps against broader policy criteria than those applied by the Competition Bureau in merger review but leaving open the question of whose assessments are determinative on purely competition-related concerns.

Third, and related, there is continuing ambiguity on the scope of the so-called regulated industries defence, which courts have held, as a matter of the constitutional division of powers, permits provincial authorities to adopt or authorize regulatory policies that would otherwise be inconsistent with provisions in the *Competition Act*. Courts have interpreted this defence broadly and have viewed even broad delegations of authority to professional or trade associations as justifying the adoption of anti-competitive regulatory policies by these associations. There is a persuasive case for a much narrower scope for the regulated industries defence, as evident in other jurisdictions such as the United States.[16]

Fourth, the division of responsibilities between the Competition Bureau (investigation and enforcement) and the Competition Tribunal (adjudication of contested cases; approval of consent orders), while well-intentioned, has not evolved as many of the framers intended. As of 2017, since its inception the Competition Tribunal has adjudicated the abuse of dominance provisions only six times and adjudicated only six contested mergers – over a period of about thirty years. While the bifurcated agency model – in separating investigation and enforcement on the one hand, and adjudication on the other – seems to have many virtues in avoiding the reality or perception of an agency being a judge in its own cause, in fact in Canada almost all competition issues are resolved within the Competition Bureau in processes that are much less transparent than the review process envisaged for the Competition Tribunal in contested cases. While it is a delicate matter, given my early membership of the Competition Tribunal, I believe that there are several reasons for the relatively minor role the tribunal has played in the administration of Canadian competition policy. First, none of the initial judicial members of the tribunal had expertise in competition law or policy, and most of the lay members also lacked any specialized expertise in the field beyond general business backgrounds. The qualifications of subsequent judicial appointees has been much stronger, and a professional economist now typically sits as a member of the tribunal. However, in the early formative years, lacking specialized expertise and experience that would have permitted wise and relatively expeditious second judgments in contested cases, the tribunal – led by its judicial members – allowed the adjudicative process to degenerate into highly protracted adversarial proceedings conducted much as in high-stakes civil litigation. This has meant, for example, that mergers, which are typically time sensitive in relations with employees, customers, and suppliers, when contested, have typically taken more than two years to resolve before the Competition Tribunal. Merger review does not have to be this way, as exemplified by the European Commission's merger review process, which in contested cases is required to be concluded within five months and takes a much more inquisitorial than adversarial form.[17]

One lesson that I have derived from the Canadian experience with the bifurcated agency model in competition law is that whatever its virtues in the abstract, actual performance depends very much on implementation factors much closer to the ground, including appointment processes and operating procedures. As one of my former deans and later president of a major North American university likes to emphasize – in part a reflection of salutary leadership experience – "Implementation, Implementation, Implementation" (as is starkly evident in faltering efforts of many governments to respond to the COVID-19 pandemic). Academics (including me), who live mostly in a world of ideas, are often insensitive to the importance of implementation issues, or worse, regard them as below their pay grade and to be resolved by lower-level functionaries. This is a serious mistake and explains why many good ideas often yield disappointing outcomes in practice. This concern also highlights the importance of institutionalized periodic reviews of the efficacy of prior reforms.

Now a new competition policy reform agenda has begun to emerge in Canada and other industrialized jurisdictions, with evidence of growing concentration levels in many industries, concerns over the dominance of the so-called tech titans in the digital markets,[18] and arguments that competition policy in many jurisdictions has adopted too narrow an efficiency perspective that ignores the role of emerging industrial structures in exacerbating inequality and undue political influence.[19]

Going forward, I also believe that there is a case for bringing consumer protection policy and competition policy into closer alignment. In many respects, they are complementary – consumer protection policy largely focuses on information failures that impair choices in competitive markets, while competition policy ensures that even with reasonably complete information, consumers do in fact have available to them a competitive range of choices among suppliers of goods and services in a given market. However, it is often insufficiently recognized that in unconcentrated markets, with low barriers to entry and exit, and often vigorous import competition (sometimes of uncertain provenance, given increasingly global supply chains), consumers' information challenges may be intensified, implying that consumer protection policy may need to be targeted on precisely those markets that raise fewest competitive concerns.[20] Conversely, in highly concentrated markets, all the information in the world is unlikely to enable consumers to exert competitive discipline on suppliers (a tension insufficiently recognized in the Adelaide Law School Consumer Credit Report).

On a final note, as with my experience with consumer credit reforms in Australia, protracted reforms of basic frameworks laws, like competition law, risk fighting yesterday's battles.

Regulation of Professional Services

While the regulation of consumer-oriented service industries fell entirely outside the remit of the Adelaide Law School committee, the extension of the Canadian *Competition Act* in 1976 to services from its previous exclusive preoccupation with product markets reflected an increasing recognition of the growing importance of the service sector in many industrialized economies. Reflecting this increasing recognition, the attorney general for Ontario, Roy McMurtry – later Chief Justice McMurtry – in 1976 appointed a three-person Professional Organizations Committee to evaluate the current regulatory framework for four self-governing professions that nominally fell within the responsibility of his ministry: accountancy, engineering, architecture, and law. He appointed to this committee as chairman Allan Leal, former dean of the Osgoode Hall Law School and deputy attorney general, J. Stephan Dupre, former chair of the Department of Political Economy at the University of Toronto, and J. Alex Corry, former principal of Queen's University and a professor of law and political science. The committee in turn appointed me as research director, and I appointed two associate research directors – Professor Carolyn Tuohy, a professor of political science at the University of Toronto with specialized expertise in health care policy, and Professor Alan Wolfson, a professor of economics at the University of Toronto, again with specialized expertise in the regulation of the health professions. Thus, the composition of the committee and the research directorate had a strong academic and interdisciplinary orientation and was manifestly not intended to provide a forum for constituency representation by the various professions. Major precipitants of the attorney general's decision to appoint a committee were long-running territorial disputes between professional accounting associations over their right to practise public accountancy (the definition of which was itself a matter of serious controversy), and a similar territorial dispute between engineers and architects over the right to assume the prime consulting role in major building projects. The attorney general apparently felt that he could not leave out his own profession, for which he had nominal oversight responsibilities, from this review – a decision that did not sit easily with the legal profession in Ontario.

As research director, along with my two associates, at the outset we retained summer law students to prepare detailed overviews of the current regulation of each of these four professions and a brief historical overview of the evolution of the current regulatory regimes, which were shared with the organized professional associations in question and revised in the light of demonstrated errors or omissions. We then prepared a short public discussion document to focus on key issues to guide future research, submissions, and consultations. This provided the basis for the commissioning of a series of analytical and policy-oriented studies by knowledgeable academics of the strengths and weaknesses of current regulatory regimes along with potential policy reforms, in part informed by comparative experience in other Canadian jurisdictions and other industrialized countries. Again, these were shared with the organized professional associations in question, and they were invited to submit written briefs in response to these research studies and thereafter to meet with the committee, with the research studies and briefs as backdrops. Some of these meetings involved vigorous exchanges between representatives of professional associations and members of the committee, revealing the intensity of professional concerns over turf protection, raising legitimate apprehensions over the role of self-regulating professional bodies in promoting the protection of consumers of their services or alternatively advancing their own interests through professional protectionism. While during the tenure of the Professional Organizations Committee, these turf wars were not as prominent in the legal profession as in the other three professions, subsequently similar debates have arisen over the case for licensing paralegals to provide a restricted range of legal services directly to the public; the case for multidisciplinary practices providing complementary legal, financial, and other services; and the case for alternative business structures facilitated by new information technology in the provision of legal services that would permit a significant range of roles for non-lawyers – developments that the legal profession in Ontario has mostly resisted, while commendably, albeit belatedly, adopting in recent years a licensing regime for paralegals.[21] Notably, reinforcing concerns I noted above about competition policy reform, the voices of consumers of professional services were rarely heard by the Professional Organizations Committee in the course of its four years of deliberations, placing an uncomfortable burden on members of the committee and the research directorate and commissioned researchers to act as surrogates for the consumer interest.

At about the midpoint of the committee's work over its four-year tenure, members of the committee took an unusual step in ad hoc public inquiries: they asked me and my two associate research directors to write and publish a staff report setting out in detail our analysis of the critical issues that had emerged from background research papers, briefs, and consultations, unconstrained by the committee's own views of these issues. This was published as a substantial book form 200-page report,[22] which then provided a backdrop and focus for further consultations by the committee with interested stakeholders and leading to the publication of the committee's own report a year or so later.[23]

The committee's recommendations quickly provided the basis for resolution of boundary conflicts between engineers and architects, but led to a final resolution of similar conflicts between professional accounting bodies only almost 30 years later, albeit largely on the basis of the committee's recommendations. In the case of the legal profession, recommendations for liberalizing rules on lawyers' advertising and contingency fees and expanding the scope of the disciplinary process beyond criminal or ethical misconduct to a more active orientation designed to redress systemic or individual patterns of incompetence were gradually acted on by the Law Society of Ontario over the ensuing years.

Reflecting on this experience, I draw several tentative lessons. First, as with other policy reform engagements with which I have been associated, the absence of a clear public and media focal point for reform efforts makes such attempts a low political priority, especially resolving turf wars among contending professional bodies, which politically exhibit a zero-sum character. Second, I believe that the four-year process that the committee engaged in was excessively protracted, driven partly by the desire of committee members to find common ground among professional bodies in conflict through extensive consultations. As in other policy reform contexts, the demand for consultations can be infinite and satisfied only by unqualified adoption of a proponent's position on all issues. Structuring both a well-focused research agenda, shared on a regular and timely basis with interested constituencies, and a tightly structured consultation process with clearly defined beginning and end points and appropriate intermediate consultation junctures are critically important strategies for a well-conducted public inquiry.

I continue to think that regulation of the vast array of professional services of importance to many consumers warrants serious policy attention. Often within and across jurisdictions, particular categories of professional services are currently regulated in dramatically different and often haphazard ways, reflecting the lack of a systematic policy framework.[24] The entire field of the regulation of professional services warrants more serious and systematic policy attention than it has received in increasingly service-intensive economies.

Property Rights and Development

Serendipity played a major role in my next major policy reform engagement and led to a major reorientation of my subsequent teaching and scholarly interests. An economist friend of mine, Jack Knetsch, was a visiting research fellow at the University of Toronto Law School in 1979–80 as part of the Law and Economics program and mentioned to me that he had seen a small advertisement in the *Economist* by a research institute in Papua New Guinea, the Institute of National Affairs (INA), seeking expressions of interest from scholars willing to undertake short visits to the country to examine land compensation issues. He had developed significant expertise on valuation issues, and he thought I could provide some value-added on institutional and procedural arrangements for assessing compensation in government expropriations. He sent off a brief letter indicating our interest and we heard nothing for many weeks, when I received a call late one night inviting the two of us to visit for three weeks in the summer of 1980, which we did. In the course of this visit and as a result of many interviews, mostly in the capital of Port Moresby, it quickly became clear to us that Papua New Guinea was grappling with a wide and complicated array of property rights issues extending well beyond land compensation issues and entailing a fundamental re-evaluation of customary conceptions of communal land ownership. We prepared a brief report outlining the landscape of issues that required much more extended analysis than our brief visit permitted, and as a result I was invited back by the INA the following year with my wife and two young sons for a six-month visit to extend our study and undertake two short additional studies on the role of state-owned enterprises in the Papua New Guinean economy, and the role of the private sector in Papua New Guinea's development trajectory. Almost immediately after arriving, representatives of the INA were invited to meet with the prime minister of Papua New Guinea, Sir Julius Chan, and several of his Cabinet ministers to discuss contemporary policy concerns. When the issue of reform of customary or communal property rights in land was raised he immediately appointed a prime ministerial task force, including me, a senior Papua New Guinean grandee who had headed up a commission several years earlier with a somewhat similar mandate, a young Papua New Guinean lawyer, and a veteran expatriate administrator with thirty years' experience with day-to-day administrative issues in the Department of Lands. Complementary backgrounds and perspectives provided for a highly congenial deliberative environment, and we were able to reach fairly detailed recommendations in just a few months on many key issues.

To set the context, Papua New Guinea is a South Pacific island complex that lies due north of Australia and just south of the equator with a population of about five million people, comprising 700 different tribes speaking many non-mutually intelligible languages. Human beings are thought to have lived in Papua New Guinea for 50,000 years, and the country contains some of the world's oldest extant preliterate cultures, which have long attracted the interest of many of the world's most distinguished anthropologists, including Bronislaw Malinowski and Margaret Mead. In the late nineteenth century different parts of the country were British and German colonies, but after the First World War the country was effectively administered as an Australian colony, becoming independent in 1975. The formal economy of Papua New Guinea prior to the Second World War was tiny in scale, involving principally copper and gold exports. After the war, the economy began to grow rapidly, with exports diversifying to include coffee, rubber, tea, lumber, fish, palm oil, and copra. Even at the time of my visits, most of the population lived in rural areas and were engaged in small-holder agriculture or subsistence food production, with very few engaged in formal employment. The country did not produce its first university graduate until 1965.

With respect to land issues, over 90 per cent of the total land area in the 1980s was customary land owned under traditional or customary title by nationals, typically through communal or group ownership regimes that varied greatly in characteristics from one tribe or clan or region of the country to another. These arrangements have often existed since time immemorial and for the most part were not subject to any written records or formal title registration regime, despite two unsuccessful efforts by the Australian colonial administration after the Second World War to formalize title to customary land across the country. Colonial-era legislation also prohibited the alienation of customary land, except in voluntary transactions with the government or through government expropriation, with the government often acting as intermediary and then leasing land acquired from custom landowning groups to private parties. With the increasing commercialization of the economy, including the agricultural sector, this highly informal and restrictive property rights regime was coming under increasing stress, manifested in a wide range of conflicts over land development projects, sometimes involving violent conflicts between adjacent tribes or clans or leaseholders.

Economists have long stressed the importance of well-defined and protected private property rights, along with effective contract enforcement, as predicates for a well-functioning market economy and have viewed communal ownership rights, coupled with severe restrictions on alienability, as inconsistent with efficient incentives for resource development. In contrast, other disciplines such as anthropology and sociology have tended to stress that such regimes in a traditional culture are embedded in much broader and culturally fundamental concepts of kinship relationships, which unconstrained private markets in land, dominated by concepts of alienable individual property rights, are likely to undermine. Papua New Guinea in the early 1980s was a classic example of the challenges that these two contrasting normative perspectives presented in formulating policy reform proposals. These were the challenges that the prime ministerial task force was charged with addressing.

We quickly became convinced that sweeping, one-size-fits-all reform proposals were entirely inappropriate in Papua New Guinea. The Papua New Guinean elder on our task force readily persuaded us that conceptions of communal ownership of land and relationships between group and individual ownership and usufructuary rights varied widely across the country, albeit rarely recorded in any form of official documentation. His knowledge of these "facts" was of enormous value to us, underscoring the point that facts, while always important, come in many different forms, and local knowledge is crucially important, while importing or transplanting policies and institutions from sharply different political, economic, and cultural contexts entails risks of discordance with the local context (as prior failed Herculean efforts at reform demonstrated). Thus, our reform proposals were animated by a spirit of incrementalism designed to facilitate new forms of land use but also to minimize social disruption from abrupt and radical policy changes (reflecting my concern with transition costs that has animated much of my subsequent thinking and writing on policy reforms, culminating in a book in 2014, *Dealing with Losers: The Political Economy of Policy Transitions*,[25] where I am critical of mainstream economists for often not taking transition costs sufficiently seriously).

In this spirit, we recommended that the scope for direct dealings in communal property be expanded to include a range of transactions such as leases, joint ventures, and mortgages, but in every case precluding outright alienability of communal property. We also recommended a tighter and better defined legal structure for landowning groups, permitting incorporation of such groups with well-defined internal decision rules by group members and their representatives. We finally recommended a rudimentary form of sporadic rather than systematic title registration, based on local land court orders, where security of title was an important prerequisite for transactions with third parties, but for communal landowning groups not contemplating such transactions no concomitant obligation or pressure to engage with the titling system.[26]

Shortly after submitting the report, the minister of lands announced that he accepted our recommendations and would be preparing draft legislation for consideration by Cabinet. Shortly after this announcement, he was fired or resigned in the face of serious corruption allegations relating to ministerial approval of government leaseholds. As I came to discover both during my visit and thereafter, this was a microcosm of disorder and dysfunction in Papua New Guinea's political and public institutions. Over the years since independence to the present day, often twenty to thirty parties, in a country with a population of about five million people, contest national elections, and governments typically comprise fragile coalitions of some subset of these parties with party and coalition membership permeable and transient, creating (as public choice theorists would predict) a policy environment where short-termism and political patronage dominate most government decisions. To this day I have not been able to establish with any confidence the fate of our policy proposals for property rights reform in Papua New Guinea or alternative reforms that may have been adopted or evaluations of their efficacy. While serendipity played an important role in my initial engagement with property rights reform in Papua New Guinea, political serendipity – mostly negative – largely determined the fate of our proposals.

In 2019, Papua New Guinea was ranked 153 out of 189 countries in the United Nations Development Program's Human Development Index, and 137 out of 180 countries in Transparency International's Corruption Perceptions Index. This, despite substantial flows of foreign aid (principally from its former colonial overseer, Australia) in the decades since independence in 1975, regular World Bank visiting missions, an endless flow of foreign consultants (such as myself), and expatriate experts recruited from offshore on limited-term contracts. My experience in Papua New Guinea led subsequently to a much more general interest in law, institutions, and development, reflected in a commitment to teaching or co-teaching upper-year seminars in law and development, often with colleagues from developing countries, and in my academic scholarship culminating in two books with a colleague and co-teacher, Mariana Prado, originally from Brazil.[27] Central to our teaching and writing in the area is the premise that the quality of the country's institutions – political, bureaucratic, and legal – are an important determinant (perhaps the most important determinant) of its development prospects – the principal lesson I took away from my initial Papua New Guinean experience in the field, although many scholars have come to appreciate how country-specific factors often yield a strong form of path dependence that presents formidable challenges for major institutional reforms.

This again underscores the point that facts come in many different forms, from big statistical data to much more qualitative micro data, each serving its own and different purpose. While qualitative data risks degenerating into anecdotes or war stories, which lawyers, particularly lawyers inculcated in the common law case-by-case system are fond of, reinforced by mass media preoccupations with human drama stories, big statistical databases pose opposing problems of losing sight of the impact or potential impact of government policies on human lives as they are lived – a shortcoming brilliantly critiqued by James C. Scott,[28] although big data and refined forms of analysis thereof are increasingly capable of yielding much more granular information. Concerns over transition costs and uncertainties over actual impacts of government policies support an approach to policy-making advocated by Andrews, Pritchett, and Woolcock,[29] which they call (awkwardly) Problem-Driven Iterative Adaptation, which fashions policy initiatives incrementally and builds in adaptive mechanisms reflecting feedback from the experience of front-line program delivery personnel and their constituents, placing a large premium on implementation dynamics. Their approach shares many similarities to frameworks that Prado and I develop in our recent book, *Institutional Bypasses*.[30]

Trade Policy Reform

Following a decade of stagflation, partly driven by oil price shocks and culminating in an economic recession, the Trudeau government in 1982 appointed its former minister of defence, minister of energy, and minister of finance, Donald Macdonald, as chairman of a royal commission on the economic union and development prospects for Canada, with a three-year reporting deadline. Macdonald was a lawyer by training, but held postgraduate degrees from Harvard and Cambridge in international law and international relations. He was supported by twelve other commissioners reflecting diverse linguistic groups, regions, business interests, organized labour, and the academy, as well as by a strong academic research directorate, which commissioned seventy background research papers, including one by me and Marsha Chandler, professor of political science at the University of Toronto and subsequently chair of the Department of Political Science, on comparative industrial policies in adjusting to trade in selected OECD countries. The commission issued a three-volume report at the end of its mandate in 1985 (with very few internal dissents on most recommendations), at which point the Liberal government had been defeated and succeeded by the Mulroney Conservative government. Despite its massively broad terms of reference, one of its principal recommendations was that the government of Canada should assign a high immediate priority to negotiating a free trade agreement with the United States, its principal trading partner. The Liberal Party, under new leadership, rejected this recommendation while conversely the Mulroney government adopted it as a central feature of its economic platform. Negotiations with the US Reagan administration were quickly initiated and culminated in a draft agreement in 1988 – the Canada-US Free Trade Agreement. The negotiations leading up to this agreement, and the agreement itself, precipitated vigorous public, political, media, and academic debate in Canada, providing the central focus for federal elections later that year, in which the Mulroney Conservatives won a comfortable majority of seats in the national Parliament.

By way of personal backdrop, I had urged my faculty in the mid-1980s to appoint a specialized international trade law scholar, given the central importance to Canada's economic future of the recently launched multilateral Uruguay Round of trade negotiations and the prospect of a comprehensive bilateral trade agreement between Canada and the United States. After an initial abortive search, the dean at the time took the view that if I felt so strongly about the matter I should teach such a course myself, notwithstanding the lack of any prior expertise in the field, but he argued that I should view it as an extension of my interest in domestic competition policy to international competition policy. From the mid-1980s on onwards, I have indeed taught or co-taught such a course, not only at the University of Toronto but at NYU Law School, Yale Law School, the University of Hong Kong Law School, and Tsinghua Law School in Beijing. In the early 1990s I was privileged to co-teach the trade course at the University of Toronto for two years with Donald MacDonald after the end of his tenure as Canadian ambassador to the United Kingdom, and subsequently for one year with Sylvia Ostry, Canada's chief negotiator at the end of the Uruguay Round, and from both of them I learned a great deal about the political economy of international trade policy. My interest in the law and political economy of international trade law and policy over the past thirty years is now reflected in a major treatise on the regulation of international trade with my former student and colleague Robert Howse and more recently introductions to international trade law.[31]

With the international trading system currently under extreme stress from US-China trade conflicts, the COVID-19 pandemic precipitating major re-evaluations of the wisdom of extensive reliance on global supply chains for essential medical supplies and access to vaccines and antivirals, and the role of international trade policy in addressing climate change, trade policy has never been more important or more contentious.

Reflecting on my engagements with this field from the mid-1980s onwards, first I have always been preoccupied with policies that mitigate the transition or adjustment costs associated with major structural changes in our economy, whether induced by trade, technology, or other factors, even where these changes are in general or in the long run socially and economically desirable.[32]

Second, I have always been struck and indeed chagrined by how difficult it is to have an intelligent and balanced debate about trade issues and broader matters of globalization, including immigration policy, without descending into the exchange of crude generalities or unhelpful broadsides or slogans. In this respect, I recall during the course of vigorous public and political debates leading up to the Canadian federal elections in 1988, which were in effect a public referendum on the Canada-US Free Trade Agreement, being frequently called by the media for snap opinions on all manner of claims being made in public fora. For example, Maude Barlow, the leader of the Council of Canadians, who was extremely active in these debates, claimed that ratification of the agreement would lead to the political, economic, and cultural assimilation of Canada into the United States, and the erosion of distinctively Canadian values. The mass media would often ask me for thirty-second soundbites for the evening news in reaction to claims such as this. Any reply that suggested a complex balance sheet of strengths and weaknesses of the 500-page agreement was viewed as simply irrelevant. Instead, my ideal response from the media's perspective would have been that the agreement would lead to the streets of Canada being paved with gold in short order, in sharp contrast to claims by Barlow and other critics of impending disaster. But this is not what I thought, and in short order I decided not to engage in the debates at this level and to decline almost all media invitations for comments. This is generally the position I have taken on most complex public policy debates subsequently, although confessing to misgivings about surrendering the public domain to proselytizers, sloganeers, instant experts, and conspiracy theorists, especially with the emergence of social media. I have become convinced that facts matter, and that evidence-based policy-making is a crucial determinant of good government, although this view is under threat from many quarters,[33] including the rise of populist political parties and their leaders, and evidenced in the erratic political commitment to scientific expertise in many countries in the contemporary COVID-19 pandemic and in responding to potentially catastrophic prospects of climate change. Indeed, in the wake of Canada-US Free Trade Agreement, despite Maude Barlow's prognostications, Canada has increasingly diverged from the United States on many aspects of social policy, including capital punishment, abortion, same-sex marriage, gun control, and universally accessible high-quality health care and education.

Third, my interest in cross-border movement of goods, services, and capital later extended to cross-border movement of people (the so-called fourth economic freedom), which has become a politically fraught issue in many countries in Europe and in the United States. This interest led me to co-author (with Ninette Kelley) a history of Canadian immigration policy,[34] and more recently to speculate on the reasons for Canadian exceptionalism in contemporary immigration policy where Canada has become in per capita terms one of the largest recipients of immigrants in the world (reflecting increasingly diverse countries of origin) and without provoking serous political or public dissension.[35] In my view, Canada's recent history of relatively liberal trade and immigration policies is a history of which Canadians can be justifiably proud in an increasingly fractious world.

Legal Aid Reform

Historically, legal aid in Ontario had been provided on a pro bono voluntary basis by individual lawyers, firms, or community-based organizations, but after the Second World War, reflecting the expansion of the welfare state, by the mid-1960s Ontario (and other provincial) governments committed themselves to public financing of legal aid services for indigent or low-income Ontarians, principally through a certificate system administered by the Law Society of Ontario pursuant to which lawyers in private practice would be remunerated, according to prescribed time and fee schedules, for representing qualifying clients and qualifying classes of matters. The certificate system was subsequently complemented by a growing number of community-based legal aid clinics, specializing either by location or class of client or matter, and currently numbering about eighty clinics distributed across the province.

In the mid-1990s, in a period of economic recession in the province and large fiscal deficits, the left-of-centre New Democratic government then in power became concerned over the escalating and open-ended legal aid budget, particularly the certificate system. In 1994, it entered into a memorandum of understanding with the Law Society of Ontario capping the legal aid budget and resulting in a reduction in the number of certificates issued by 150,000 per year. In late 1996, the recently elected Conservative government, through its attorney general, appointed a seven-person task force chaired by John McCamus, former dean of the Osgoode Hall Law School, to conduct a fundamental re-evaluation of the current legal aid program and to propose recommendations for reform. Task force members, including one judicial member, were reflective but not formal representatives of a broad range of constituencies or backgrounds implicated in the provision of legal aid services. In turn, Professor McCamus appointed me as research director of the task force. We began our work in early 1997 and completed the substance of our work about eight months later with a three-volume report being published later that year. In the course of our work we received 170 written submissions; I commissioned some twenty or so background research papers; and members of the task force met with a large range of groups across the province. These meetings were typically chaired by Professor McCamus, while my responsibilities lay principally in overseeing the research program, with frequent interactions between Professor McCamus and me on issues arising in the public meetings that required attention in the background research papers, or issues raised by the researchers that would benefit from ventilation and discussion in public meetings.

The deliberations amongst members of the task force in reaching its key recommendations and endorsing a unanimous report were highly congenial – although sometimes spirited – and quickly led to the enactment by the Ontario legislature of the *Legal Services Act 1999* that implemented most of the recommendations of what came to be known as the "McCamus Report" – appropriately so, given his masterful oversight of the task force's deliberations and his deft personal and political skills in managing interactions with a wide range of external constituencies. The report led to the creation of a new independent public agency, Legal Aid Ontario, superseding the administrative role previously played by the Law Society of Ontario, with appointments to the agency to be made by the attorney general of Ontario reflecting a set of criteria designed to ensure representation of a wide range of perspectives in the administration of the legal aid program, while avoiding the potential risks of conflict and perhaps gridlock in a constituency-based board of governance. The new legislative framework, reflecting the recommendations of the McCamus task force, accorded primacy to the certificate system in the areas of criminal law and family law while encouraging the new agency to be innovative in exploring new delivery models in these two areas and other areas of law with major impacts on indigent or low-income Ontarians.

In 2007, the attorney general of Ontario in a Liberal government asked Professor McCamus to review the efficacy of the reforms implemented in 1999, along with recommendations for further reforms if necessary, but his appointment as chair of Legal Aid Ontario precluded him from doing more than an initial launch of the review. In turn, the attorney general asked me in August 2007 to undertake this review, which I did over the following six months, submitting a detailed report to the attorney general in February 2008, and publicly released by the attorney general five months later in August 2008[36] (after some pressure from interested constituencies). In the course of preparing my report, I met with thirty-three associations or groups and thirteen individuals. As with the McCamus Report, and as indeed with the Professional Organizations Committee deliberations some three decades earlier, at an early stage I made publicly available a short discussion document to focus the issues under consideration.

In my report, I generally concluded that the new governance arrangements had worked reasonably well and did not call for radical change. I was somewhat critical of the new agency for not being sufficiently innovative or experimental in exploring new delivery models, and in particular more integrated service modalities that recognized that individuals with legal problems often also faced a range of other challenges that were not well dealt with by a silo-based delivery system. I was also critical of successive governments for not augmenting the financial base of the new agency, and in particular for not expanding financial eligibility criteria for over a decade, despite increases in the cost of living, and also for not implementing a systematic periodic tariff review regime for the certificate system, where again prescribed hourly rates had been allowed to decline in real terms, reflected in a declining percentage of the practising profession, especially in family law and criminal law, being prepared to accept legal aid certificates.

To its credit, the government of the day, despite an economic recession in the province, committed itself to enhancing Legal Aid Ontario's budget by $50 million a year, although the current government has substantially reduced its budget. A number of my other recommendations on innovation and experimentation with alternative delivery modalities received serious attention from the agency itself. The *Legal Aid Services Act* (2020) reaffirms the importance of Legal Aid Ontario exploring innovative delivery modalities for legal aid services.

In general, and in retrospect, I regard my two policy review engagements with the legal aid system in Ontario as amongst my most productive and satisfying public policy involvements, and have led to an enduring scholarly interest in access to justice.[37]

Electricity Sector Reform in Ontario

From early in the twentieth century, the electricity sector in Ontario has been dominated by a state-owned public utility, Ontario Hydro, which was initially charged with acquiring privately owned generation facilities in the province and assuming responsibility for building new generation capacity and developing a province-wide transmission network, while leaving local distribution functions to mostly municipally owned local utilities. In performing these functions,

Ontario Hydro was rarely far from the political limelight, given that the impact of its decisions was reflected in highly visible and frequent bills for electricity charges to industrial, commercial, and residential consumers, as well as intense controversies from the 1960s onwards about the cost and environmental implications of large-scale investments in nuclear power generation.

In the early 1990s, in large part reflecting these costs, the retail price of electricity increased by 30 per cent, leading the government of the day, in the face of intense consumer reactions, to impose a price freeze that remained in force until 2002. As of 1999, Ontario Hydro was carrying $20 billion in stranded provincially guaranteed debt that could not be serviced and retired in a competitive electricity sector. Following the election of a Conservative government in 1995, an advisory committee appointed under the chairmanship of Donald Macdonald (the same Donald Macdonald) recommended that the province move to a more market-oriented electricity sector, in particular with respect to generation and energy retailing, recognizing that transmission and local distribution were effectively natural monopolies that required some form of regulation. The government released a White Paper in 1997 proposing full wholesale and retail competition by 2000 and the division of Ontario Hydro into its generation and transmission components, which subsequently occurred in 1999 when Hydro One was created to own and operate the transmission grid, and Ontario Power Generation was created to own and operate the generation assets.

The White Paper led to the creation of the Market Design Committee (MDC) in 1998, charged with responsibility for designing and recommending rules for wholesale and retail competition in the province's electricity market. My former student, colleague, co-teacher, co-author, and then dean of the University of Toronto Faculty of Law and subsequently president of Johns Hopkins University, Ron Daniels, was appointed chair and executive director of the MDC, along with two associate executive directors, Professor Donald Dewees of the Department of Economics at the University of Toronto, and John Grant, a retired investment banker. The committee itself comprised representatives of all the major stakeholder groups – Ontario Power Generation, Hydro One, independent generators, large industrial consumers, commercial consumers, residential consumers, and environmentalists – a committee of about fourteen members.

The executive director in turn appointed me as research director, and we immediately launched an international search for a specialized consulting firm with extensive comparative experience in electricity sector reform. To this end we hired a fairness consultant and a major Canadian law firm to advise us on the structuring of the search process and the terms of the several million dollar consulting contract that we entered into with the successful firm, whose senior personnel were located full-time in Toronto for all of 1998 during the tenure of the MDC, and would prove to be an invaluable source of technical expertise and advice to the committee.

With a constituency-based committee, questions naturally arose at the outset about the decision rules that would govern the committee's deliberations, with some media commentators predicting an early implosion of a committee comprising interests that historically were often highly adversarial. At an early meeting, the chairman/executive director announced that the committee's deliberations would be governed by a "substantial consensus" rule, which meant more than a bare majority in favour of any particular recommendation or proposal but less than unanimity, and he was adept at avoiding further precision, except to note that in the event of an absence of substantial consensus on any given issue, the default rule would not be paralysis but a decision would be taken by the three members of the executive directorate and me as research director (advised by our international consultants).

Over the course of the year of the MDC's deliberations in 1998, a vast array of technically complex and politically sensitive issues were debated and with few exceptions resolved by a substantial consensus. The committee met almost weekly for full days Fridays and reported as directed by the government with a full set of detailed recommendations running to some 300 pages by the end of 1998.

Further to the government's prior commitment to full wholesale and retail competition, the committee developed detailed rules governing both, but paid particular attention to the challenge of moving from a near OPG monopoly in the generation sector (then 90 per cent of generation capacity) to something that more credibly resembled a competitive market structure. The government was acutely aware of the political sensitivities surrounding full-scale privatization of what were widely seen as provincial Crown jewels previously vested in Ontario Hydro and now divided between

Ontario Power Generation and Hydro One, but both still fully state-owned (successive Liberal governments later partly privatized Hydro One to institutional investors).

The MDC wrestled with various dimensions of this issue for several months and in the end recommended that within three and a half years of market opening, OPG should be required to divest itself of 65 per cent of its price-setting generating units, and 65 per cent of its core or baseload facilities within ten years of market opening. Until these targets were met, under the Market Power Mitigation Agreement that the MDC proposed, and that the government and OPG accepted, OPG would be required to pay a rebate to consumers on 90 per cent of its domestic sales when the wholesale price exceeded 3.8 cents per kilowatt hour. The MDC also recommended the creation of an independent market operator (IMO) to operate the spot market and the dispatch function and to undertake continuing market surveillance for irregularities or distortions in the wholesale market, while remitting to the Ontario Energy Board the function of regulating transmission and local distribution charges (and subsequently the market surveillance function, which was transferred from the IMO, now the Independent Electricity System Operator).

The wholesale market was initially scheduled to open in 2000, but logistical challenges faced by both the IMO and private sector participants in operationalizing the new regime resulted in a significant delay, and the market finally opened on 1 May 2002. This delay proved to be significant because in the intervening two years California, which had undertaken a somewhat similar process of market-oriented reforms to its electricity sector, had experienced some seriously dysfunctional and unanticipated consequences, and the major US electricity trading company, Enron, had gone bankrupt. Both events had induced major private investor misgivings about investments in the electricity sector. Moreover, in Ontario, various nuclear generation plants were out of commission and were subject to unscheduled delays in reinstatement, creating uncertainties for Ontario's generation capacity at the time of market opening, despite a highly positive assessment by the IMO prior to market opening that sufficient generation capacity was available to meet all reasonable demand projections.

When the market opened, the average hourly wholesale price was 3.01 cents per kilowatt in May and 3.71 cents in June. Thereafter, in one of the hottest summers in Ontario on record, prices began to increase rapidly, and in July the average hourly energy price was 6.2 cents, with a dramatic expansion of demand as consumers turned on their air conditioning, and severe constraints emerged on the supply side with less water for hydro generation, reduced nuclear capacity, and congestion on interties with neighbouring Quebec, Manitoba, New York, Michigan, and Minnesota. In the face of increasingly hostile consumer reactions to their escalating electricity bills, and prominent media focus, the new leader of the Conservative Party, facing the prospect of an election the following year, announced in November 2002 that his government would freeze most retail prices at 4.3 cents per kilowatt retroactive to market opening. Following the election of a Liberal government late the following year, a dizzying and never-ending stream of ad hoc interventions in the Ontario electricity market followed, often in the form of ministerial directives from an ever-changing cast of ministers of energy, with most wholesale prices now regulated either under government contracts or Ontario Energy Board oversight and the Market Power Mitigation Agreement abandoned. The retail price freeze in its various permutations has meant that the government has had to assume fiscal responsibility for differences between wholesale and retail prices, which it has passed on to consumers in less transparent form in something mysteriously called the Global Adjustment, or transferred onto the general body of taxpayers – a form of fiscal illusion. The fixed retail prices have muted incentives for consumers to conserve on electricity consumption; and the unstable and ad hoc nature of policy interventions has deterred private investment in the sector, at least unless supported by long-term fixed price government contracts.

The experiment with wholesale price competition in the Ontario electricity sector lasted little more than six months. After the work of the MDC was completed at the end of 1998, we collectively received an award from the Institute of Public Administration of Canada for the best conducted regulatory review in the previous year. However, our sense of self-satisfaction or even self-congratulation proved short-lived. What went wrong?[38]

Serendipity obviously played a major role, given the timing of market opening following shortly on the heels of the California electricity market meltdown and the Enron bankruptcy; the unscheduled outages of nuclear plants in Ontario and delays in their reinstatement; and one of the hottest summers on record. But this concatenation of events should not preclude a searching self-critique.

With the benefit of hindsight, the MDC might have taken a different position on various issues. For example, we could have recommended an immediate breakup of Ontario Power Generation into six or eight entities and their privatization thereafter, but I seriously doubt that any political party had the appetite for this kind of bolder prescription. We might have spent less time on the complicated rules governing retail energy competition. We might have been more aggressive in forcing dramatic consolidation of the 300 mostly municipally owned local distribution entities (now reduced to about 80, mainly as a result of Hydro One acquisitions), so that they could have served the function of counter-parties or load-serving entities in entering into long-term bilateral contracts with existing or prospective generation operators. But municipalities were vehement in their opposition to any such forced consolidation, viewing their local distribution companies as cash cows and a convenient venue for patronage appointments by local politicians. We might have taken more seriously the need to create a capacity market or to impose capacity reserve requirements on existing generators to mitigate the risk of capacity shortfalls in the system instead of taking the IMO's forecast at face value.

These are all speculative afterthoughts, and looking back over the year of MDC deliberations (masterfully orchestrated by its chairman), in my view they were highly professional and highly productive, and reflected great integrity in a commitment by all participants (with all the compromises involved in reaching a substantial consensus) to design the features of a better electricity system for Ontario, recognizing the dysfunctional features of the pre-existing system, and now with the benefit of hindsight in knowing the continuous state of disorder that came after the failed reforms. An important role played by the Executive Committee, the external consultants, and the Research Directorate, in an otherwise constituency-based committee, was to compel constituents to attempt to justify self-interested positions within a well-specified mandate and hence to discipline accordingly cruder interest group politics.

It would be remiss of me not to comment briefly on a prominent feature of the subsequent Liberal government's electricity policies: the enactment of the *Green Energy Act* in 2009, which in the broader context of concerns over climate change was intended to reduce greenhouse gas emissions in the electricity sector by promoting renewable energy, principally in the form of wind and solar, while phasing out coal-fired generation (achieved in 2014).[39] The objective of the *Green Energy Act* was to ensure that renewables would account for at least 10 per cent of generation capacity in the medium term, an objective to be advanced by offering renewable energy developers fixed-price twenty-year contracts with the Ontario Power Authority, a new government electricity procurement agency. The price of power for wind turbines was set at 13.5 cents per kilowatt hour, while solar power qualified by up to 80 cents per kilowatt hour. In 2009, the average wholesale cost of electricity was around 6 cents per kilowatt hour. How these prices were arrived at has never been explained. However, they provoked a corporate feeding frenzy, suggesting that competitive tendering would have generated substantial savings for the province (as the auditor general subsequently found). Despite early assurances from the minister of energy and his supporters that these policies would have a trivial impact on consumers' electricity bills, the effect was dramatic, with estimates finding that between 2008 and 2017 the average increase in the price of the energy component in electricity prices in Ontario was 107 per cent compared to an increase in the consumer price index over this period of 17.8 per cent. Given the modest contribution of electricity generation in Ontario (the bulk of it hydro and nuclear) to greenhouse gas emissions, following the phasing out of coal-fired generation and its replacement principally with natural gas–fired generation, these policies seem also to have had a very modest impact on greenhouse gas emissions. And claims that they would generate a whole new renewable energy industry in Ontario entailing 50,000 new jobs seem to have had little or no foundation. In provincial elections in 2017, the Liberal Party was thrown out of office and reduced to a rump in the Ontario legislature without official party status. The saga of the electricity sector reform in Ontario has no end in sight.

The only significant academic pay-off from this disillusioning engagement has been an ongoing scholarly interest in the role of state-owned enterprises (SOEs) in the economies of both developed and developing countries – an issue of major significance, particularly for the latter, whose SOEs have been much more prominent features of their economies than in the former.[40]

Future Role of Government in Ontario

In January 2002, the premier of Ontario's Conservative government announced the formation of a panel to study the future role of government in Ontario (primarily on the initiative of the premier's chief political advisor), with the redoubtable Ron Daniels as chairman and seven panellists. He in turn appointed me as research director, and I hired two full-time research associates (Andrew Green and Roy Hrab, both with law and economics orientations). Over the course of the next year and a half, we commissioned forty-four research papers by highly respected academics on a vast array of topics reflecting trends that we expected to emerge in Ontario over the next ten to fifteen years, including an aging population and implications for the health care sector, a continuing influx of immigrants from around the world needing assistance in many cases in integrating into the Ontario economic and social context, continuing rural-urban immigration with major growth of urban centres and a hollowing out of the economic and social infrastructure of many rural communities, changes in the structure of the Ontario economy reflecting an increasing prominence of the service sector, the changing structure of labour markets and implications for the educational and training sectors, new demands on physical infrastructure, particularly public transit in expanding urban centres, and the revitalization of public engagement in political processes, provincial and local, in addressing many of these challenges.

In the meantime in mid-2002, Premier Harris announced that he would not be seeking a third term, precipitating a change in leadership of the Conservative Party and the temporary suspension of our activities until our mandate was confirmed by the new leader. The chairman, I, and our two research associates then prepared a detailed 240-page staff report synthesizing much of the research that we had commissioned on the theme "Creating a Human Capital Society for Ontario." The panel found this report too detailed to form the basis of their own report and instructed us to prepare a much shorter version touching on many of the issues noted above (and more). The panel's 80-page report was submitted in February 2004, after the election of a Liberal government in late 2003, and was released by the new premier in April 2004.[41] The chairman in his letter of submission reported that the panel incurred expenditures of $1.5 million against a committed budget of $1.8 million and that the panel estimated that its recommendations would entail additional annual government expenditures of $2.7 billion, which could be accommodated within the prevailing fiscal framework with recommended tax and expenditure reforms. Both the report and the background research papers quickly disappeared from public sight. As far as I am able to judge, little of our work has had any demonstrable impact on subsequent government policies.

In retrospect, both Ron Daniels and I were foolhardy in undertaking this engagement. The terms of reference for the panel was so expansive and diffuse that they lacked clear focal points that the public and mainstream media could relate to. Because our mandate directed us to look at emerging trends ten to fifteen years out, issues lacked contemporary political salience; and the change in political leadership of the

Conservative Party and then the change of government meant that there was no committed political patron or promoter of the panel's deliberations and recommendations. Obviously, the new government had little incentive to credit any of its policy platform or initiatives to deliberations initiated by the prior government, although it did adopt a strong education/training policy orientation, including full-day junior and senior kindergarten (as recommended by the panel).

The panel's composition and subsequent internal dynamics were also unsatisfactory in many respects. A majority of the panel were long-serving provincial civil servants who were inclined to extreme caution in recommending bold new policy initiatives that reflected concerns over straining relations with past, present, or future political masters, while another panellist took the view that little new research was required because all the important emerging policy issues and their resolution were clear and could be quickly articulated, creating tensions with the research staff. In the end, the panel produced a relatively short report that did insufficient justice to the substantial body of research that we had commissioned and insufficiently focused on clear, actionable near-term policy prescriptions. While many of the research papers were presented in draft at workshops at the University of Toronto to fellow researchers and invited individuals with a special interest or expertise in the topic under discussion, the panel was also resistant to broad and prompt dissemination of background research papers to relevant constituencies for their reactions, or to embark on any systematic public consultations with these constituencies, thus attenuating any public engagement with the panel's deliberations.

I continue to believe that much of the research commissioned on behalf of the panel was of high quality and addressed many important emerging policy issues in Ontario and deserved much broader ventilation. In retrospect, perhaps a blue sky panel with major thinkers in the central policy areas under review would have served a more useful long-term public purpose in getting major new ideas out into the public domain and perhaps prompting the development of new veins of promising policy-oriented research, largely abstracting from any direct or immediate impact on the policy-making process, but perhaps over time broadening the policy horizons and being available as a policy resource in the event that future political critical junctures raised their salience.

PART C

Lessons Learned (the Hard Way)

I now attempt to pull together some threads from the foregoing, rather eclectic set of personal engagements with the public policy-making process, beginning in Australia, but focused predominantly on Canada and more particularly the province of Ontario, and relate some of the lessons I have learned from these engagements to positive theories of the public policy-making process canvassed in part A of this book.

Serendipity

Serendipity, for better or worse, has played a major role in a number of my public policy engagements, being favourable in terms of time and place in the case of the Adelaide Law School committee's report on consumer credit, despite our modest credentials, and being unfavourable in intervening events in the Electricity Market Design Committee: the California market meltdown, the Enron bankruptcy, logistical delays in market opening, and one of the hottest summers on record after market opening, and being unfavourable in the Future Role of Government Panel with a change in the leadership of the Conservative government and then a change of government before the panel's report was concluded.

Harold Macmillan, Conservative prime minister of the United Kingdom from 1957 to 1963, was once said to have remarked in response to a question of what factors were most likely to throw a government off course, "Events, my boy, events." His successor as prime minister, Labour Party leader Harold Wilson, once remarked that "a week is a long time in politics" (manifestly not the case for most academics). For academics who engage in the public policy-making process, as I have done, this is a hard and painful lesson to learn. Scholars, in developing, testing, and refining new ideas, often incubate them over a period of years and debate them in rarefied academic workshops, symposia, and conferences far from the policy front lines. The academic and real-world policy environments in many respects could not be more different.

Short-Termism

Closely related to the role of serendipity in the public policy-making process is short-termism. At least in liberal democracies, political parties are elected to government typically in four- or five-year electoral cycles and, as public choice theorists have emphasized, public policies adopted or promised within each cycle must be chosen with a view to maximizing the prospects of re-election at the end of the cycle. Thus, policies that impose substantial short-term costs on salient political constituencies with deferred or uncertain long-term benefits carry significant political risks. However, as Alan Jacobs has persuasively argued,[1] political parties in government often do adopt policies that entail very long-term horizons where consistent with their political survival. For example, they may make substantial investments in health care and educational infrastructure, physical infrastructure such as roads and public transit systems, parks, and museums, and public pension systems. Thus, it is important not to oversimplify the incentive structures facing politicians, as discussed in part A of this book. However, policies that involve substantial up-front costs and highly uncertain and deferred long-term benefits (climate change policy being the most prominent contemporary example) present formidable challenges for democratically elected governments, in contrast to policies that spread costs and benefits broadly over people and over time where governing parties may have more policy latitude and the scope for factional politics is more limited, although the long slog associated with reform of basic framework laws and policies that lack immediate political salience often reflect government reluctance to draw down on scarce political capital without commensurate discernible political returns.

Policy-Oriented Ad Hoc Public Inquiries

For purposes of the following discussion, I distinguish forward-looking policy-oriented public inquiries of the kind that I have been associated with from backward-looking inquisitorial public inquiries designed to make findings of culpability for past human scandals or tragedies, along with hybrid versions of both kinds of inquiries.

Terms of Reference

Ideally, the terms of reference of policy-oriented public inquiries should be well focused, should identify key issues to be explored, and should be tractable in time frame and resources so that the agenda is reasonably clear to all affected parties from the outset.

Leadership

In policy-oriented ad hoc public inquiries, it is a truism that, as with many other forms of collective human endeavour, leadership matters. While differing in many personal respects, the leadership qualities exhibited by John McCamus in the Legal Aid Task Force, Donald Macdonald in the Macdonald Royal Commission of Inquiry into Canada's Future Economic Prospects, and Ron Daniels in the Electricity Market Design Committee shared important characteristics: high intelligence, high integrity, and deft political and interpersonal skills. This combination of characteristics is far rarer than one might suppose.

Composition

It is also a truism that the composition of the membership of an ad hoc policy-oriented committee of inquiry is a crucial determinant of its effectiveness. In this respect, there is no simple set of prescriptions. One option is to appoint a small committee of respected and disinterested experts in the general policy field in question, along the lines of the Professional Organizations Committee, even if they lack specialized expertise in the particular issues in contention. This option carries a significant obligation of extensive consultations with affected constituencies, ideally both on the supply and demand sides of the issues in question, recognizing

that for some constituencies there can never be enough consultation unless their view prevails. This option also carries
a significant obligation of undertaking relevant research
by recognized experts on specific issues in question on the
nature and efficacy of existing policies and future policy
alternatives. Such background research needs to be made
available in a timely fashion to all affected constituencies so
that they can address research findings and recommendations in submissions and consultations.

A contrasting option is to design the committee membership on a formal constituency basis, with major supply-side
and demand-side interests formally designating representatives to serve on the committee, very much along the lines
of the Electricity Market Design Committee (sometimes
called regulatory negotiation or "reg-neg"). One risk with
this option is policy deadlock if the designated constituencies hold sharply divergent positions (as they often will).
This risk can be mitigated by a tight committee mandate –
in the electricity case, designing the rules for a competitive
wholesale and retail electricity market – and can be further
leavened by the choice of decision rules governing the committee's deliberations – in the electricity market design,
the adoption of a substantial consensus rule and a default
rule that the executive committee would resolve issues that
could not be resolved by a substantial consensus against a
well-defined mandate that precluded unconstrained asser-
tions of relative political influence. An advantage of this
option is that it largely internalizes the consultation process
in that the major affected constituencies are already represented on the committee, although there is a residual risk of

discounting the interests of those who are not represented or weakly represented (for example, final consumers).

An intermediate option reflected in the Legal Aid Task Force, the Macdonald Royal Commission, and the Future Role of Government Panel is for the government of the day to appoint members to the committee who reflect a range of perspectives and backgrounds that to some extent reflect in microcosm the diversity of perspectives and backgrounds in the polity at large. With this option, members of the committee are not formal representatives of organized constituencies but act in their personal capacities. In the interests of transparency and accountability, a proactive public consultation and research program is likely to be important with this intermediate option – successful in the Legal Aid Task Force, and much less successful in the Future Role of Government Panel.

Process

As to process, particularly in the first and third options, I have often served as research director – sometimes effectively chief of staff – for the policy-oriented ad hoc public inquiries with which I have been associated. Reflecting on this role, it is clear that I lacked specialized prior expertise in many of these public policy engagements. Rather, I saw my role as an ideas broker or intermediary soliciting the participation and contributions of the best scholars available from different perspectives and ensuring that their background research studies met acceptable standards of rigour and lucidity, and that the public policy implications of their research were clearly spelled out. In another respect, I also saw my role as a broker or intermediary between the world of ideas and the world of interests – constituencies or stakeholders who considered their interests directly engaged by the public policy inquiry we were mandated to conduct. While complete congruence or convergence of views between these two worlds is often an unrealistic aspiration, narrowing differences of opinion on key issues is often a realistic aspiration

To this end, I have come to think that an idealized process might unfold roughly as follows: First, at the outset of a committee or panel's mandate – ideally well focused and tractable – research staff and committee or panel members should conduct a quick and informal set of consultations or reconnaissance with members of the relevant scholarly communities and affected constituencies and stakeholder groups to identify the key policy issues (but not their resolution) that the committee or panel should focus on in its deliberations, with a view to producing a short discussion paper early in its mandate. This paper might be distributed in draft to scholarly contacts and affected constituencies for brief and expeditious reactions before formal release – a process that in its entirety should not take more than about three months.

Following the release of this discussion document, background research papers should be commissioned from a variety of perspectives on the key issues identified in the discussion document. Many of these research studies will not entail original research but rather a synthesis of the best existing research on the issues in question. Empirical evidence may entail large databases describing broad economic and social trends that provide a backdrop to the policy issues under analysis or much more fine-grained data that provide a sense of flesh-and-blood experience of lives lived under existing policies or alternative policies where comparative experience is available. As I noted earlier, big databases risk discounting this important dimension of policy design and implementation, while focusing only on flesh-and-blood experiences of lives lived risks policy-making by anecdote, although analysis of large databases is now becoming sufficiently refined to yield quite granular findings. As I have emphasized in earlier comments, relevant facts come in many shapes and sizes, and an important role for the research director of the policy-oriented public inquiry, and his or her staff, is to ensure that members of the committee or panel are presented with background research that synthesizes relevant empirical evidence of different kinds.

Background research should also reflect a range of credible normative perspectives on policy implications drawn or proposed by the commissioned researchers. No discipline has more than a partial grasp on all the determinants of human well-being. Modesty in the claims made on behalf of any disciplinary perspective is an important quality – not a characteristic prominently associated with either of the disciplines that I have most seriously engaged with: law and economics. Lawyers often are preoccupied with process over substance; economists with broad welfare judgments that abstract from more granular impacts of given policies on subsets of the population, insensitivity to transition costs, and a predilection for notoriously unreliable economic forecasting (which John Kenneth Galbraith once remarked made astrology seem respectable).

Integration of diverse perspectives is a rare academic quality[2] and places a premium on generalists who can traverse specialized disciplinary domains (not always regarded as an academic virtue).[3]

To take the case of the COVID-19 pandemic, medical experts can make judgments, based on prevailing scientific evidence, of factors that exacerbate or mitigate the risk of infection and responses to it, but not the economic or psychological costs of protracted isolation policies or the developmental impact of home schooling on children, etc. For better or worse, we rely on our political institutions, with all their frailties, to weigh all these perspectives in generating and frequently refining a complex set of policy responses.[4]

As a general matter, these background research papers should generally be completed, at least in draft, within about six months of commissioning. In the meantime, following the release of the discussion paper, affected constituencies and stakeholder groups should be invited to make written submissions to the committee or panel within about three months, with submissions being made available, as relevant, to commissioned background researchers. Members of the committee or panel, or subsets of it, might also schedule informal consultations with representatives of affected constituencies or stakeholder groups following receipt of written submissions. As draft background research papers are completed, they should be promptly and broadly disseminated to affected constituencies and stakeholder groups for short and expeditious comments before being finalized for public release. Key draft background research papers might also be discussed fruitfully in research workshops to which members of the committee or panel would obviously be invited, along with relevant members of the research community and affected constituencies or stakeholder groups.

At this juncture, probably nearing the one-year point from the beginning of its mandate, members of the committee or panel should have available to them a substantial corpus of background research and submissions from affected constituencies and stakeholder groups that is inclusive in the constituencies engaged and expansive in the normative perspectives canvassed and empirical and comparative evidence deployed. Synthesizing and structuring this corpus of material around key themes in broadly accessible form and tractable length is a major challenge, which in the first instance is probably best assigned to the research director and his or her staff, in close consultation with the chair of the panel or committee, in many cases yielding a staff report to members of the panel or committee. The core elements of this report might form the basis of a final round of informal consultations by members of the committee or panel, or subsets of it, with representatives of affected constituencies or stakeholder groups. At this juncture, members of the committee or panel, ideally led by the chair of the committee or panel, need to turn their minds to the structure and form and key recommendations of their own report. Realistically, writing the report cannot be a collective endeavour and it is likely to be assigned to the research director and staff in close consultation with the chair and under the general direction of the committee.

Following a process roughly in accordance with that described above, most policy-oriented ad hoc public inquiries should rarely extend beyond a tenure of two years and can sometimes feasibly be concluded within a shorter time (as in the Legal Aid Task Force Report).

Investigative/Hybrid Ad Hoc Public Inquiries

Investigative/hybrid ad hoc public inquiries have been a common phenomenon over the course of Canada's history, typically precipitated by a political or related scandal or human tragedy such as contaminated blood, contaminated municipal water supplies, freight train derailments in urban centres resulting in chemical spills in surrounding communities, passenger airliners blowing up in mid-air as a result of a suspected bomb placement, etc. Typically, public and media outcry demand an investigation of events leading up to the scandal or tragedy and the assignment of blame or culpability for its occurrence. Such inquiries are often undertaken by a single judge experienced in conducting criminal and civil trials. Often such inquiries implicate a large volume of documents, a large number of witnesses, and a large number of lawyers representing parties either as potential culprits or actual or potential victims. In sharp contrast to policy-oriented ad hoc public inquiries, the process employed in investigative public inquiries has tended to be highly formalized and highly adversarial, reproducing the features of criminal or civil trials in many respects.

However, seriously complicating the nature of investigative ad hoc public inquiries is the potential admixture of human wrongdoing or delinquencies and systemic failures that have facilitated such wrongdoing or delinquencies and whose reform engages much more with the nature of a forward-looking policy-oriented ad hoc public inquiry.

While I have not personally been involved directly in such public inquiries, I and my colleague Lisa Austin have analysed in detail one such prominent inquiry, headed by Mr. Justice Horace Krever of the Ontario Court of Appeal (and formerly a legal academic specializing in health law and policy) between 1993 and 1997 into failures of the Canadian blood system, then administered by the Canadian Red Cross, which led to several thousand Canadians contracting either HIV-AIDS or hepatitis C from blood transfusions as a result of failures to screen blood donors and test blood samples adequately.[5] At the outset of this inquiry, Mr. Justice Krever stated, "It is not and it will not be a witch hunt. It is not concerned with criminal or civil liability." The inquiry was initially scheduled to take two years and entail government expenditures of $2.5 million. In fact, it took four years and entailed an expenditure of $17.5 million. He conducted 247 days of hearings, which involved fifty-three lawyers, 474 witnesses, and 175,000 documents.

In contrast, Lisa Austin and I in our analysis note that also in 1993, the US secretary of the Department of Health and Human Services asked the Institute of Medicine, a highly respected medical research institute, to examine similar issues that had arisen in the United States and to recommend steps to prevent or reduce the risk of their recurrence. The Institute of Medicine, in turn, established a committee of fourteen members charged with reviewing and evaluating the safety of the US blood system and recommending reforms to it. The institute report was completed in June 1995 and was unanimously endorsed by all fourteen members of the committee and was published later that year by the National Academy press as a 335-page book, divided into eight chapters, containing fourteen principal recommendations, which led to reforms to the American blood system. In contrast to the Krever Commission of Inquiry, the Institute of Medicine study spent $685,000, held two days of public hearings, which involved no lawyers, heard from seventy-two witnesses, reviewed over 700 documents, and spent seventeen months from its inception until the publication of its final report. This is a stunning contrast. The IOM was not given the responsibility for assigning blame or culpability to actors in the pre-existing US blood system, leaving issues of blame or culpability to be resolved in subsequent civil proceedings – for example, class actions by victims, or possibly although less plausibly subsequent criminal proceedings. However, it bears reiteration that Mr. Justice Krever himself disclaimed any responsibility for making findings of the kind that might be appropriate in civil or criminal proceedings.

The central dilemma raised by investigative ad hoc public inquiries is that issues of individual wrongdoing and systemic failures cannot be disentangled. A human tragedy of the kind exemplified in the blood system inquiries in Canada, the United States, and elsewhere might reflect any of the following scenarios: (1) good systems impaired or compromised by bad individuals; (2) bad systems disabling or undermining good individuals; (3) bad systems attracting and being reinforced by bad individuals. Any public inquiry into human tragedies of this kind, in principle, needs to unravel these individual-systemic connections and make recommendations for systemic reforms that make the underlying systems more resilient to risks of human failings of the kind at issue in the particular inquiry or other risks that may compromise the efficacy of the system in question. However, recommendations for systemic reforms of this kind implicate precisely the kind of future-oriented policy reform ad hoc public inquiry described above and ideally implicate similar processes of inquiry, in stark contrast to the adversarial processes employed to assign blame or culpability ("naming and shaming" or "who did what to whom"). Moreover, generalist judges who may be highly competent and experienced in overseeing adversarial criminal or civil trials may seldom be nearly as qualified to play the leadership role, or indeed exclusive role, in evaluating and recommending reforms to complex underlying systems. As I and Lisa Austin argue in our analysis of the Krever Commission's proceedings, while lawyers specialize in a vast range of different areas of law, they typically share a commitment to the rule of law, which in turn they too commonly conceptualize as entailing highly adversarial trial-type processes, while most decisions in life by families, communities, and nations typically entail radically different decision-making processes. After all, Winston Churchill declared war on Germany at the outset of the Second World War following a Cabinet decision to that effect, but without a two- or three-year civil trial involving numerous witnesses and counsel and voluminous documentary discovery. I believe that the processes that I have described above for conducting a policy-oriented ad hoc public inquiry fully conform to functional notions of due process and their emphasis on participation, transparency, and accountability.

Since the Krever Commission, some investigative ad hoc public inquiries have done a much better job of partitioning the naming-and-blaming function and systemic reform portion of such inquiries, and disciplining tightly the former and broadly following the kind of processes I described above with respect to the latter. The Walkerton Inquiry into contaminated municipal water supplies, conducted by Mr. Justice Dennis O'Connor of the Ontario Court of Appeal (and culminating in reports in 2002), is an exemplary case in point. However, concerns will arise about the qualifications and credibility of a single judge in such cases to undertake responsibility for systemic evaluation and proposed reforms – concerns that can be met only by appointing a multi-member commission with relevant and diverse backgrounds or appointing a strong research staff and perhaps advisory committees on systemic issues and a proactive multidisciplinary consultation process.[6]

Positive Theories of the Public Policy-Making Process Revisited

In general, I believe that my personal engagements with the public policy-making process where ideas, interests, and institutions intersect confirm many of the implications of positive theories of this process canvassed in part A of this book.

The process is much less deterministic and more fluid than austere public choice theories would imply and in many contexts is shaped by vagaries, serendipities, or personalities that defy easy theorizing. However, public choice theory still offers some salutary lessons: the tendency by political decision-makers to over-weight short-term costs and benefits and discount longer-term costs and benefits of policy choices in many contexts; the tendency to over-weight the influence and representations of concentrated producer interests and discount diffuse final consumer interests (at least when not reasonably proxied by intermediaries); high sensitivity to contemporary political salience, which in turn is often the product of random events and their purchase with various constituencies, increasingly articulated through social media, rendering public policy-making more of a random walk or at best "muddling through" (in Charles Lindblom's famous phrase)[7] than most scholars are likely to find congenial; and relatedly an increasing disparagement of evidence-based policy analysis and expertise more generally as elitist among many segments of the population – a trend exacerbated by social media where fact, fiction, fantasy, falsehood, bubbles, and echo chambers are subject to few of the disciplining forces associated with traditional epistemic communities and reflected in the rise of populist political movements and increased political and social polarization in many countries.[8] The role of scholars in the public policy-making process in this environment will often be contentious and often (for them) a source of disillusionment, but also a reality check on those given to unhelpful forms of utopianism.

Concluding Thoughts

Reviewing my engagements as an academic within the public policy-making process over the course of a long career, it will be obvious that this is not a self-aggrandizing exercise in moving from one policy triumph to another, but rather a very mixed balance sheet of the occasional success, a number of failures, and often long slogs, even where some positive policy impacts were eventually realized.

At the end of such a career, one might self-critically ask whether there are better ways for scholars to spend their time. A sharply different scholarly paradigm is the "attic academic" – the attic could be anywhere – who spends years pondering and refining complex new ideas, while interacting with a small circle of sympathetic or critical fellow scholars, in the hope that at some point the intellectual product of this relative intellectual seclusion will be a paradigm shift in the way that scholars generally conceive of a particular issue and then ultimately the public at large or at the very least the policy elite. A few scholars in any discipline achieve this dream, but most do not and are largely resigned to seeing their life's work gathering dust in libraries or appearing in arcane specialized academic publications that attract a handful of readers. I do not disparage such scholars. Over the course of human history, some such scholars have changed the way much of the world thinks about issues of central importance to humanity. Notwithstanding the oft-quoted claim of John Maynard Keynes that "sooner or later it is ideas, not vested interests, which are dangerous for good or evil,"[9] the chances of most scholars having this kind of impact are remote.

For my part, I took what I thought was a safer bet: given my intrinsically functional or instrumental mindset, to try to make the world a slightly better place in incremental ways in the here and now, and for the most part as an idea broker or intermediary, which sometimes yielded personal academic spin-offs in the form of ideas of my own that I developed from my brokerage role and the privileged access that it provided to me to the worlds of ideas and interests in important public policy contexts. Whether this was the most socially productive use of my time, typically at public expense, I leave others to judge. In the meantime, for academics (such as myself) who choose to engage with the real-world policy-making process, with all its frustrations, frailties, and foibles, it is useful to remind ourselves first that there is no obviously superior system on offer.[10] Important policy challenges – often novel and complex – are unremitting and unavoidable. New policy challenges abound, many of which are likely to be addressed, in the Canadian tradition, by ad hoc commissions of inquiry or government task forces (in which academics are likely to often be engaged), including post-mortems on what went well or badly in the handling of the COVID-19 pandemic and how we can prepare better for the future pandemics; appropriate policies for Canada to adopt to meet the challenge of climate change and transition costs associated with such policies;[11] reform of framework laws and policies such as competition laws, privacy laws, intellectual property laws, and employment laws to address the impact of technological innovations, including artificial intelligence; and changing configurations of international trade and investment in a world of rapid technological change and increasing geopolitical factionalism. Public inquiries, when well conceived, well structured, and well conducted have at least the potential to modestly ameliorate tendencies to denigrate evidence-based policy-making in our contemporary world. To recall a quip by Daniel Patrick Moynihan, distinguished American scholar and former US senator, "Every-one is entitled to their own opinions, but not to their own facts."

However, public inquiries should aspire to do more than merely provide authoritative factual matrices for the status quo and policy alternatives to it (important as that is). They need also to embrace in their research agenda a broad range of credible normative perspectives and adopt a proactive, inclusive public consultation process where a broad range of citizens are, in the words of Nobel Laureate Amartya Sen,[12] engaged as active "agents" and not merely as passive "patients" in the policy-making process ("government by discussion"). In these ways, public inquiries, at their best, may help shape a public consensus on ways forward in addressing some of our most challenging public policy issues.

Notes

Introduction

1 Michael J Trebilcock, "Reform of the Law Relating to Consumer Credit" (1970) 7 *Melbourne UL Rev* 315; Michael J Trebilcock, "The Rogerson Report Twenty-One Years Later" (1990) 3 *Corporate & Bus LJ* 103; Anthony Duggan, "Consumer Credit Redux" (2010) 60 *UTLJ* 687.

2 Michael Trebilcock & Francesco Ducci, "The Evolution of Canadian Competition Policy: A Retrospective" (2018) 60 *Can Bus LJ* 171.

3 Michael Trebilcock, Carolyn Tuohy, & Alan Wolfson, *Professional Regulation*, Staff Study (Toronto: Government of Ontario, 1979); *Report of the Professional Organizations Committee* (Toronto: Government of Ontario, 1980).

4 Michael J Trebilcock, "Communal Property Rights: The Papua New Guinean Experience" (1984) 34 *UTLJ* 377.

5 Michael Trebilcock, Douglas Hartle, Robert Prichard, & Don Dewees, *The Choice of Governing Instrument* (1982) Economic Council of Canada, Working Paper.

6 Carolyn J Tuohy & Michael J Trebilcock, *Policy Options in the Regulation of Asbestos-Related Health Hazards* (Royal Commission on Asbestos, 1982).

7 Bruce Chapman & Michael J Trebilcock, "Making Hard Social Choices: Lessons from the Auto Accident Compensation Debate" (1992) 44 *Rutgers L Rev* 797.

8 Marsha Chandler & Michael Trebilcock, "The Political Economy of Economic Adjustment: The Base of Declining Sectors," research paper

1986. See subsequently Michael Trebilcock, Marsha Chandler, & Robert Howse, *Trade and Transitions* (London: Routledge, 1990).

9 Michael Trebilcock, Melody Martin, Anne Lawson, & Penney Lewis, "Testing the Limits of Freedom of Contract: Commercialization of Reproductive Technologies and Materials" (1994) 32 *Osgoode Hall LJ* 613.

10 McCamus Task Force, *Report of the Ontario Legal Aid Review: A Blueprint for Publicly Funded Legal Services*, 3 vols (Toronto: Government of Ontario, 1997).

11 Michael Trebilcock, *Report of Legal Aid Review* (Toronto: Ontario Ministry of the Attorney General, 2008).

12 Michael J Trebilcock & Roy Hrab, "Electricity Restructuring in Canada" in Fereidoon P Sioshansi & Wolfgang Pfaffenberger, eds, *Electricity Market Reform: An International Perspective* (Oxford: Elsevier, 2006); Michael Trebilcock, "Ontario's Green Energy Experience: Sobering Lessons for Sustainable Climate Change Policies" (15 August 2017), online: CD Howe Institute, https://www.cdhowe.org/sites/default/files/attachments/research_papers/mixed/e-brief_263.pdf.

13 Panel on the Role of Government, *Investing in People: Creating a Human Capital Society for Ontario* (2004).

14 Anita Anand, ed, *What's Next for Canada? Securities Regulation After the Reference* (Toronto: Irwin Law, 2012).

15 See Michael Trebilcock, *The Limits of Freedom of Contract* (Cambridge, MA: Harvard University Press, 1993), chap. 10 (for a discussion of similar issues in contract law).

Part A: The Role of Ideas, Interests, and Institutions in the Canadian Policy-Making Process

1 See Michael Trebilcock, *The Prospects for Reinventing Government* (Toronto: CD Howe Institute, 1994).

2 Michael Trebilcock, Douglas Hartle, Robert Prichard, & Donald Dewees, *The Choice of Governing Instrument* (1982) Economic Council of Canada, Working Paper.

3 See Michael Trebilcock, "The Choice of Governing Instrument: A Retrospective," in Pearl Eliades, Margaret Hill, & Michael Howlett, eds, *Designing Government* (Montreal & Kingston: McGill-Queen's University Press, 2005); Michael Trebilcock, *Dealing with Losers: The Political Economy of Policy Transitions* (New York: Oxford University Press, 2014), chap. 2.

4 Louis Kaplow & Steven Shavell, *Fairness versus Welfare* (Cambridge, MA: Harvard University Press, 2006).

5 Arthur Ripstein, "Critical Notice: Too Much Invested to Quit," Book Review of *Fairness versus Welfare* by Louis Kaplow and Steven Shavell (2004) 20 *Economics and Philosophy* 185; Guido Calabresi, *The Future of Law and Economics: Essays on Reform and Recollection* (New Haven, CT: Yale University Press, 2016).

6 Michael Trebilcock & Douglas Hartle, "The Choice of Governing Instrument" (1982) 2 *Intl Rev Law & Econ* 29.

7 Daniel Kahneman, *Thinking Fast and Slow* (New York: Farrar, Straus and Giroux, 2011); Dan Ariely, *Predictably Irrational* (New York: Harper Collins, 2008).

8 Cass R Sunstein, *How Change Happens* (Cambridge, MA: MIT Press, 2019); Duncan Green, *How Change Happens* (Oxford: Oxford University Press, 2016); Leslie Crutchfield, *How Change Happens: Why Some Social Movements Succeed While Others Don't* (Hoboken, NJ: John Wiley & Sons, 2018); Jonathan Haidt, *The Righteous Mind: Why Good People Are Divided by Politics and Religion* (New York: Pantheon Books, 2012); Ezra Klein, *Why We're Polarized* (New York: Avid Reader Press, 2020).

9 Paul Pierson, "Increasing Returns, Path Dependence, and the Study of Politics" (2000) 94 *American Political Science Rev* 251; Douglass North, *Institutions, Institutional Change, and Economic Performance* (Cambridge: Cambridge University Press, 1990); Michael Trebilcock & Mariana Prado, "Path Dependence Theory, Economic Development and the Dynamics of Institutional Reform" (2009) 59 *UTLJ* 341.

10 See, e.g., B. Guy Peters, *Institutional Theory in Political Science: The New Institutionalism*, 4th ed (Cheltenham, UK: Edward Elgar, 2019); Trebilcock, *Dealing with Losers*, chap. 2.

11 Donald Savoie, *Democracy in Canada: The Disintegration of Our Institutions* (Montreal & Kingston: McGill-Queen's University Press, 2019); Donald Savoie, *Governing from the Centre: The Concentration of Power in Canadian Politics* (Toronto: University of Toronto Press, 1999).

12 See Trebilcock, Hartle, Prichard, & Dewees, *The Choice of Governing Instrument*, chap. 4.

13 House of Commons, Canada, List of Committees, https://www .ourcommons.ca/Committees/en/List; Senate of Canada, Committees: https://sencanada.ca/en/Committees/.

14 See, for instance, CES Franks, *The Parliament of Canada* (Toronto: University of Toronto Press, 1987); Christopher Raymond & Jacob Holt, "Due North? Do American Theories of Legislative Committees Apply to Canada?" (2014) 20:2 *J Legislative Studies* 174; Helene Helboe Pedersen, Darren Halpin, & Anne Rasmussen, "Who Gives Evidence to Parliamentary Committees? A Comparative Investigation of Parliamentary Committees and Their Constituencies" (2015) 21:3 *J Legislative Studies* 408; Michael Rush, "Studies of Parliamentary Reform – Parliamentary Committees and Parliamentary Government: The British and Canadian Experience" (1982) 20:2 *J Commonwealth & Comparative Politics* 138; Paul Thomas, "The Influence of Standing Committees of Parliament on Government Legislation (1978) 3:4 *Legislative Studies Q* 683; CES Franks, "The Dilemma of the Standing Committees of the Canadian House of Commons" (1971) 4:4 *Can J Political Science / Revue Canadienne De Science* Politique, 461.

15 Marguerite Marlin, "Interest Groups and Parliamentary Committees: Leveling the Playing Field" (2016) 39:1 *Canadian Parliamentary Rev* 24.

16 House of Commons, Canada, House of Commons Procedure and Practice, Committees, https://www.ourcommons.ca/About/ProcedureAndPractice 3rdEdition/ch_20_4-e.html.

17 See, for example, discussion in Mark Winfield, "The Role of Parliamentary and Legislative Committees in Canadian Environmental Policy Development and Evaluation: The Case of the House of Commons Standing Committee on Environment and Sustainable Development 1994–2004" (2010) 22:1 *J Envtl L & Prac* 59.

18 *An Act Respecting Public and Departmental Inquiries*, RSC 1985, c I-11 [Federal *Inquiries Act*].

19 The British government began to form royal commissions pertaining to Canada in the 1800s. See Thomas J Lockwood, "A History of Royal Commission" (1967) 5:2 *Osgoode Hall LJ* 172 at 172.

20 *Ibid* at 198.

21 Gregory Inwood & Carolyn M Johns, "Why Study Commissions of Inquiry" in Inwood & Johns, eds, *Commissions of Inquiry and Policy Change: A Comparative Analysis* (Toronto: University of Toronto Press, 2014) at 7. The official federal government website listed 370 commissions. For a full list, see https://www.canada.ca/en/privy-council/services/commissions -inquiry.html.

22 Federal *Inquiries Act*.

23 *Ibid*, s 2.

24 Ontario *Public Inquiries Act*, s 5.

25 *Ibid*, ss 8–10.

26 Federal *Inquiries Act*, s 4; Ontario *Public Inquiries Act*, s 10.

27 Federal *Inquiries Act*, s 11; Ontario *Public Inquiries Act*, s 26.

28 Federal *Inquiries Act*, s 13; Ontario *Public Inquiries Act*, s 17(1).

29 Federal *Inquiries Act*, s 12; Ontario *Public Inquiries Act*, s 17(2).

30 Ed Ratushny, *The Conduct of Public Inquiries* (Toronto: Irwin Law, 2009) at 24.

31 *Ibid* at 15.

32 Madam Justice Freya Kristjanson, "Procedural Fairness and Public Inquiries" in Ronda Bessner & Susan Lightstone, eds, *Public Inquiries in Canada: Law and Practice* (Toronto: Thomson Reuters, 2017) at 98–103.

33 *Chrétien v Gomery*, 2008 FC 802, aff'd 2010 FCA 283.

34 See, e.g., *Stevens v Canada (AG)*, 2004 FC 1746.

35 Ed Ratushny, *The Conduct of Public Inquiries* (Toronto: Irwin Law, 2009) at 5.

36 The British government began to form royal commissions pertaining to Canada in the 1800s. See Lockwood, "History of Royal Commissions" at 172.

37 Commission of Inquiry into the Air Ontario Crash at Dryden, Ontario (the "Moshansky Commission"); Commission of Inquiry into the Investigation of the Bombing of Air India Flight 182 (the "Major Commission").

38 Commission of Inquiry into the Deployment of Canadian Forces to Somalia (the "Somalia Inquiry"); the Oliphant Commission, see discussion under section B.

39 David Pacciocco, "Taking a 'Goudge' out of Bluster and Blarney: An 'Evidence-Based Approach' to Expert Testimony" (2009) 13 *Can Crim LR* 135 at 152.

40 Canada, Department of Justice, "Criminal Liability for Workplace Deaths and Injuries: Background on the *Westray Law*" (2019), online: *Department*

of Justice, https://www.justice.gc.ca/eng/rp-pr/other-autre/westray/p1.html.

41 Thomas R Berger, "Canadian Commissions of Inquiry: An Insider's Perspective" in Allan Manson & David Mullan, eds, *Commissions of Inquiry: Praise or Reappraise* (Toronto: Irwin Law, 2003) at 14–15.

42 Genevieve Cartier, "Research and Policy in a Public Commission of Inquiry" in Ronda Bessner & Susan Lightstone, eds, *Public Inquiries in Canada: Law and Practice* (Toronto: Thomson Reuters, 2017) at 231–232. The Supreme Court of Canada has similarly observed that commissions of inquiries have "wide-ranging investigative powers," which put them in a better position than the judiciary to examine all the surrounding circumstances and to "take a long-term view of the problem presented": *Phillips v Nova Scotia (Commission of Inquiry into the Westray Mine Tragedy)*, [1995] 2 SCR 97 at 62.

43 Ed Ratushny, *The Conduct of Public Inquiries* (Toronto: Irwin Law, 2009) at 2–3.

44 Joan Grace, "Politics and Promise: A Feminist-Institutionalist Analysis of the Royal Commission on the Status of Women" in Gregory J Inwood & Carolyn M Johns, eds, *Commissions of Inquiry and Policy Change: A Comparative Analysis* (Toronto: University of Toronto Press, 2014) at 83–84.

45 Gregory J Inwood & Carolyn M Johns, "Commissions of Inquiry and Policy Change: A Comparative Analysis" in Inwood & Johns, eds, *Commissions of Inquiry and Policy Change: A Comparative Analysis* (Toronto: University of Toronto Press, 2014) at 265.

46 The Supreme Court of Canada has praised the commissions of inquiry for playing an important educative role, noting that "[t]hey are an excellent means of *informing and educating concerned members of the public*" and "[b]oth the status and high public respect for the commissioner as well as the open and public nature of the hearing help to *restore public confidence* not only in the institution or situation investigated but also in the process of government as a whole": *Phillips v Nova Scotia (Commission of Inquiry into the Westray Mine Tragedy)*, [1995] 2 SCR 97 at paras 62–64.

47 Ontario, *Report of the Walkerton Inquiry, Part One: The Events of May 2000 and Related Issues* (Toronto: Ministry of Attorney General, 2002) (Commissioner: The Honourable Dennis R O'Connor) at chap 14.3.

48 *Ibid.*

49 See Sherry Glied, "Policy Analysis in Government and Academia: Two Cultures" (2018) 43 *J Health Pol Pol'y & L* 537.

50 Ronald L Watts, "The Macdonald Commission Report and Canadian Federalism" (1986) 16:3 *The State of American Federalism* 175 at 178.

51 Robert Centa & Patrick Macklem, "Securing Accountability Through Commissions of Inquiry: A Role for The Commission of Canada" in Allan Manson & David Mullan, eds, *Commissions of Inquiry: Praise or Reappraise* (Toronto: Irwin Law, 2003) at 96–98.

52 *Beno v Canada (Commissioner and Chairperson, Commission of Inquiry into the Deployment of Canadian Forces to Somalia)*, [1997] 1 FC 911, 126 FTR 241 (TD),

rev'd [1997] 2 FC 527 (AD); *Dixon v Canada (Somalia Inquiry Commission)*, [1997] 3 FC 169, 1997 CarswellNat 1133 (AD) rev'g [1997] 3 FC 169 (TD) [*Dixon*]; *Boyle v Canada (Somalia Inquiry Commission)* (1997), 131 FTR 135, [1997] FCJ No 942 (TD); *Morneault v Canada (AG)* (1998), 150 FTR 28, [1998] FCJ No 501 (TD), rev'd (2000), 184 FTR 15 (AD); *Labbé v Canada (Somalia Inquiry Commission)* (1997), 128 FTR 291, 1997 CarswellNat 325 (TD).

53 *Dixon v Canada (Somalia Inquiry Commission)*, [1997] 3 FC 169, 1997 CarswellNat 1133 (AD) rev'g [1997] 3 FC 169 (TD).

54 *Canada (AG) v Canada (Commission of Inquiry on the Blood System)*, [1997] 3 SCR 4404.

55 *MacKeigan v Hickman*, [1989] 2 SCR 796.

56 *Solicitor General of Canada, et al v Royal Commission (Health Records)*, [1981] 2 SCR 494.

57 Gregory J Inwood & Carolyn M Johns, "Commissions of Inquiry and Policy Change: A Comparative Analysis" in Inwood & Johns, eds, *Commissions of Inquiry and Policy Change: A Comparative Analysis* (Toronto: University of Toronto Press, 2014) at 257.

58 Among the factors contributing to this lag is cost. See Gregory J Inwood & Carolyn M Johns, "Commissions of Inquiry and Policy Change: Comparative Analysis and Future Research Frontiers" (2016) 59:3 *Canadian Public Administration* at 395.

59 Aaron Wherry, "Another Doctor Is In: Philpott Joins Bennett in Pursuit of Reconciliation," *CBC News* (28 August 2017).

60 See discussion under section B.

61 Federal *Inquiries Act*, ss 12–13; Ontario *Public Inquiries Act*, s 5. Furthermore, despite the legal existence of a right to representation, in practice, the absence of a guarantee of funding for legal representation, such that exists in criminal trials, certain affected individuals may, in practice, face economic barriers to afford representation.

62 Justice John H Gomery, "The Pros and Cons of Commissions of Inquiry" (2006) 51:4 *McGill LJ* 783 at 790, 792; A Wayne MacKay, "Mandates, Legal Foundations, Powers and Conduct of Commissions of Inquiry" in A Paul Pross & Innis Christie, eds, *Commissions of Inquiry* (Toronto: Carswell, 1990) at 37.

63 *Ibid*.

64 Bryan Schwartz, "Public Inquiries" in Allan Manson & David Mullan, eds, *Commissions of Inquiry: Praise or Reappraise* (Toronto: Irwin Law, 2003) at 448.

65 Ed Ratushny, *The Conduct of Public Inquiries* (Toronto: Irwin Law, 2009) at 105.

66 Indeed some scholars have noted that governments, rather, face a political disincentive to form a commission because they must surrender a degree of control over its policy agenda or its ability to shape public opinion in relation to the subject matter of investigation to the independent commissions. See Robert Centa & Patrick Macklem, "Securing Accountability Through Commissions of Inquiry: A Role for The Commission of

Canada" in Allan Manson & David Mullan, eds, *Commissions of Inquiry: Praise or Reappraise* (Toronto: Irwin Law, 2003) at 92.

67 Speaking a number of years later, Justice Gilles Letourneau, the chair of the Somalia Commission, reiterated the independence of the commission, noting that while a commission of inquiry is not independent in the sense that it "receives its budget from the government" and "it works for the government," it is independent in the pursuit of its terms of reference on a day-to-day basis, and it certainly has the freedom to think and form its own opinions. Tamar Witelson, "Interview with Mr. Justice Gilles Letourneau" in Allan Manson & David Mullan, eds, *Commissions of Inquiry: Praise or Reappraise* (Toronto: Irwin Law, 2003) at 361–362, 367.

Part B: Personal Reflections on Engagements with the World of Ideas and Interests in Public Inquiries

1 Anthony Duggan, "Consumer Credit Redux" (2010) 60 *UTLJ* 687.

2 Michael Trebilcock, "The Rogerson Report Twenty-One Years Later" (1990) 3 *Corporate & Bus LJ* 103.

3 Duggan, "Consumer Credit Redux."

4 Donald Dewees, David Duff, & Michael Trebilcock, *Exploring the Domain of Accident Law: Taking the Facts Seriously* (New York: Oxford University Press, 1996); see also Michael Trebilcock & Jeremy Fraiberg, "Risk Regulation: Technocratic and Democratic Tools for Regulatory Reform" (1998) 43 *McGill LJ* 825.

5 Richard Susskind, *Tomorrow's Lawyers* (City: Oxford University Press, 2012); Edward Iacobucci & Michael Trebilcock, "An Economic Analysis of Alternative Business Structures in the Provision of Legal Services" (2014) *Can Bar Rev* 57.

6 See, e.g., Michael Trebilcock, Anita Anand, & Francesco Ducci, "Financial Advisors and Planners in Search of Regulatory Principles" (2020) 63 *Canadian Business LJ* 1.

7 See Michael Trebilcock, *Paradoxes of Professional Regulation: In Search of Regulatory Principles* (Toronto: University of Toronto Press, 2022).

8 Duggan, "Consumer Credit Redux."

9 See Michael Trebilcock, "Winners and Losers in the Modern Regulatory System: Must the Consumer Always Lose?" (1975) *Osgoode Hall LJ* 417.

10 Economic Council of Canada, *Interim Report on Competition Policy* (1969).

11 Lawrence A Skeoch & Bruce C McDonald, *Dynamic Change and Accountability in a Canadian Market Economy* (Ottawa: Minister of Supply and Services, Canada, 1976).

12 David McQueen, J Bruce Dunlop, & Michael J Trebilcock, *Canadian Competition Policy: A Legal and Economic Analysis* (Toronto: Canada Law Book, 1987).

13 Michael Trebilcock, Ralph Winter, Paul Collins, & Edward Iacobucci, *The Law and Economics of Canadian Competition Policy* (Toronto: University of Toronto Press, 2002).

14 Michael Trebilcock & Francesco Ducci, "The Evolution of Canadian Competition Policy: A Retrospective" (2018) 60 *Can Bus LJ* 171.

15 See Kent Roach & Michael Trebilcock, "Private Enforcement of Competition Laws" (1996) 34 *Osgoode Hall LJ* 462.

16 See Michael Trebilcock, "Regulated Conduct in the Competition Act" (2005) 41 *Can Bus LJ* 492.

17 Michael Trebilcock & Lisa Austin, "The Limits of the Full-Court Press: Of Blood and Mergers" (1998) 48 *UTLJ* 1; Neil Campbell, Hudson Janisch, & Michael Trebilcock, "Rethinking the Role of the Competition Tribunal" (1997) 76 *Can Bar Rev* 297.

18 See, e.g., Francesco Ducci, *Natural Monopolies in Digital Platform Markets* (Cambridge: Cambridge University Press, 2020).

19 Michael Trebilcock & Francesco Ducci, "The Revival of Fairness Discourse in Competition Policy" (2019) *Antitrust Bulletin* 79; Michael Trebilcock and Francesco Ducci, "The Multifaceted Nature of Fairness in Competition Policy" (October 2017) *CPI Antitrust Chronicle*.

20 See Cory Coglianese, Adam Finkel, & David Zaring, eds, *Import Safety: Regulatory Governance in the Global Economy* (Philadelphia: University of Pennsylvania Press, 2009).

21 See Michael Trebilcock, "Prices, Costs, and Access to Justice," in Trevor Farrow and Les Jacobs, eds, *The Justice Crisis* (Vancouver: UBC Press, 2020), 25.

22 Michael J Trebilcock, Carolyn J Tuohy, & Alan D Wolfson, *Professional Regulation: A Staff Study of Accountancy, Architecture, Engineering and Law in Ontario*, prepared for the Professional Organizations Committee, Ontario Ministry of the Attorney General, 1979.

23 *Report of the Professional Organizations Committee* (1980).

24 Michael Trebilcock, *Paradoxes of Professional Regulation: In Search of Regulatory Principles* (Toronto: University of Toronto Press, 2022).

25 Trebilcock, *Dealing with Losers.*

26 For a fuller elaboration of these proposals, see Michael Trebilcock, "Communal Property Rights: The Papua New Guinean Experience" (1984) 34 *UTLJ* 377.

27 Michael Trebilcock & Mariana Prado, *Advanced Introduction to Law and Development*, 2nd ed (Cheltenham, UK: Edward Elgar, 2021); Mariana Mota Prado & Michael Trebilcock, *Institutional Bypasses: A Strategy to Promote Reforms for Development* (Cambridge: Cambridge University Press, 2019).

28 James C Scott, *Seeing Like a State* (New Haven, CT: Yale University Press, 1998).

29 Matt Andrews, Lant Pritchett, & Michael Woolcock, *Building State Capability: Evidence, Analysis, Action* (New York: Oxford University Press, 2017).

30 Prado & Trebilcock, *Institutional Bypasses.*

31 Michael Trebilcock, Robert Howse, & Antonia Eliason, *The Regulation of International Trade*, 4th ed (London: Routledge, 2012); Michael Trebilcock & Joel Trachtman, *Advanced Introduction to International Trade*, 2nd ed (Cheltenham, UK: Edward Elgar, 2020); Michael Trebilcock, *Navigating the Free Trade–Fair Trade Fault-Lines* (Cheltenham, UK: Edward Elgar, 2021).

32 Michael Trebilcock, Marsha Chandler, & Robert Howse, *Trade and Transitions* (London: Routledge, 1990); Trebilcock, *Dealing with Losers*; Michael Trebilcock & Sally Wong, "Trade, Technology and Transitions: Trampolines or Safety Nets for Displaced Workers?" (2018) 37 *J International Economic Law* 1; Trebilcock, *Dealing With Losers*.

33 See, e.g., Jonathan Rauch, *The Constitution of Knowledge: In Defence of Truth* (Washington, DC: Brookings Institution Press, 2021); Tom Nicols, *The Death of Expertise: The Campaign Against Established Knowledge and Why It Matters* (New York: Oxford University Press, 2017); Cass Sunstein, *Liars: Falsehoods and Free Speech in an Age of Deception* (New York: Oxford University Press, 2021).

34 Ninette Kelley & Michael Trebilcock, *The Making of the Mosaic: A History of Canadian Immigration Policy*, 2nd ed (Toronto: University of Toronto Press, 2010).

35 Michael Trebilcock, "The Puzzle of Canadian Exceptionalism in Contemporary Immigration Policy" (2019) 20 *J Intl Migration & Immigration* 823.

36 Michael Trebilcock, *Review of Ontario Legal Aid Program*, report prepared for the Ministry of the Attorney-General, Government of Ontario, March 2008.

37 See, e.g., Michael Trebilcock, Anthony Duggan, and Lorne Sossin, eds, *Middle Income Access to Justice* (Toronto: University of Toronto Press, 2012); and Michael Trebilcock, "Price, Costs, and Access to Justice," in Trevor Farrow and Lesley Jacobs, eds, *The Justice Crisis* (Vancouver: UBC Press, 2020) 25.

38 See Michael Trebilcock and Roy Hrab, "Electricity Restructuring in Ontario," (2005) 20 *Energy J* 123; Michael Trebilcock and Roy Hrab, "Electricity Restructuring in Ontario," Fereidoon Sioshansi and Wolfgang Pfaffenberger, eds, *Electricity Market Reform: An International Perspective* (Oxford: Elsevier, 2006) 419.

39 See Michael Trebilcock, "Ontario's Green Energy Experience: Sobering Lessons for Sustainable Climate Change Policies" (15 August 2017) CD Howe Institute E-Brief.

40 See Edward Iacobucci and Michael Trebilcock, "The Role of Crown Corporations in the Canadian Economy: An Analytical Framework" (March 2012) Policy Study, University of Calgary School of Public Policy; Mariana Prado and Michael Trebilcock, *Advanced Introduction to Law and Development*, 2nd ed (Cheltenham, UK: Edward Elgar, 2020), chap 11.

41 Panel on the Role of Government, *Investing in People: Creating a Human Capital Society for Ontario* (2004).

Part C: Lessons Learned (the Hard Way)

1 Alan Jacobs, *Governing for the Long Term* (New York: Cambridge University Press, 2011).

2 For outstanding examples of successful exercises of such integration by economists, see Amartya Sen, *Development as Freedom* (New York: Alfred Knopf, 1999); and Sen, *The Idea of Justice* (New York: Belknap Press, 2009);

and more recently Abhijit V Banerjee and Esther Duflo, *Good Economics for Hard Times* (New York: Public Affairs, 2019).

3 See David Epstein, *Range: Why Generalists Triumph in a Specialized World* (New York: Riverhead Books, 2019).

4 See Fareed Zakaria, *Ten Lessons for the Post-Pandemic World* (New York: WW Norton, 2020).

5 Michael Trebilcock and Lisa Austin, "The Limits of Full Court Press: Of Blood and Mergers" (1998) 48 *UTLJ* 1.

6 See more, generally, David Moscop, *Too Dumb for Democracy?* (Fredericton, NB: Goose Lane Editions, 2019).

7 Charles Lindblom, "The Science of Muddling Through" (1959) 19 *Public Administration* 79.

8 See Jonathan Rauch, *The Constitution of Knowledge: In Defence of Truth* (Washington, DC: Brookings Institutions Press, 2021); Tom Nichols, *The Death of Expertise: The Campaign Against Established Knowledge and Why It Matters* (New York: Oxford University Press, 2017); Cass Sunstein, *Republic: Divided Democracy in the Age of Social Media* (Princeton, NJ: Princeton University Press, 2017).

9 John Maynard Keynes, *The General Theory of Employment, Interest, and Money* (London: MacMillan, 1936) at 386.

10 Michael Trebilcock, *The Prospects for Reinventing Government* (Toronto: CD Howe Institute, 1994).

11 See Edward Iacobucci and Michael Trebilcock, "Existential Threats: Climate Change, Pandemics, and Institutions," Working Paper, University of Toronto Faculty of Law, 19 December 2021.

12 See Amartya Sen, *Development as Freedom* (New York: Alfred Knopf, 1999); Sen, *The Idea of Justice* (Cambridge, MA: Harvard University Press, 2009).

Index

UTP insights

Books in the Series

- Raisa B. Deber, *Treating Health Care: How the System Works and How It Could Work Better*
- Jim Freedman, *A Conviction in Question: The First Trial at the International Criminal Court*
- Christina D. Rosan and Hamil Pearsall, *Growing a Sustainable City? The Question of Urban Agriculture*
- John Joe Schlichtman, Jason Patch, and Marc Lamont Hill, *Gentrifier*
- Robert Chernomas and Ian Hudson, *Economics in the Twenty-First Century: A Critical Perspective*
- Stephen M. Saideman, *Adapting in the Dust: Lessons Learned from Canada's War in Afghanistan*
- Michael R. Marrus, *Lessons of the Holocaust*
- Roland Paris and Taylor Owen (eds.), *The World Won't Wait: Why Canada Needs to Rethink Its International Policies*
- Bessma Momani, *Arab Dawn: Arab Youth and the Demographic Dividend They Will Bring*
- William Watson, *The Inequality Trap: Fighting Capitalism Instead of Poverty*
- Phil Ryan, *After the New Atheist Debate*
- Paul Evans, *Engaging China: Myth, Aspiration, and Strategy in Canadian Policy from Trudeau to Harper*